# GRAN PARADISO
## ALTA VIA 2 TREK AND DAY WALKS

## About the Author

Gillian Price was born in England but moved to Australia when young. After taking a degree in anthropology and working in adult education, she set off to travel through Asia and trek the Himalayas. The culmination of her journey was Venice where, her enthusiasm fired for mountains, the next logical step was towards the Dolomites, only hours away. Starting from there, Gillian has been steadily exploring the mountain ranges and flatter bits of Italy and bringing them to life for visitors in a series of outstanding guides for Cicerone. An ardent promoter of public transport to minimise environmental impact, she is an active member of the Italian Alpine Club (Club Alpino Italiano) and Mountain Wilderness. When not out walking with Nicola, her Venetian cartographer husband, Gillian works as a freelance travel writer (www.gillianprice.eu).

### Other Cicerone guides by the author

*Across the Eastern Alps: E5*
*Alpine Flowers*
*Italy's Sibillini National Park*
*Italy's Stelvio National Park*
*Shorter Walks in the Dolomites*
*The Tour of the Bernina*
*Through the Italian Alps*
*Trekking in the Alps (contributor)*
*Trekking in the Apennines*
*Trekking in the Dolomites*
*Walking and Trekking on Corfu*
*Walking in the Central Italian Alps*
*Walking in the Dolomites*
*Walking in Sicily*
*Walking in Tuscany*
*Walking on Corsica*
*Walking on the Amalfi Coast*
*Walking the Italian Lakes*
*Walks and Treks in the Maritime Alps*

# GRAN PARADISO
## ALTA VIA 2 TREK AND DAY WALKS

by

Gillian Price

# CICERONE

JUNIPER HOUSE, MURLEY MOSS,
OXENHOLME ROAD, KENDAL, CUMBRIA LA9 7RL
www.cicerone.co.uk

© Gillian Price 2018
Third edition 2018
ISBN: 978 1 85284 923 8
Second edition 2008
First edition (entitled *Walking in Italy's Gran Paradiso*) 1997

Maps and diagrams by Nicola Regine
Photos by Gillian Price and Nicola Regine
Printed in China on behalf of Latitude Press Ltd
A catalogue record for this book is available from the British Library.

## Dedication
To Nicola (who else?) with all my love

## Acknowledgements
For little Bet and little Dave, as well as Alastair, Giacomo, James, Kate, Kieran and Morgan, all big enough to carry their own rucksacks (and their aunty's) now.

Thanks to Nicola once more for his patient labour on the maps and diagrams. For this second edition I was also lucky to have the help of Gran Paradiso park ranger Roberto Cristofani and colleagues who provided precious suggestions. My keen walking companions from visits past and recent were Piero, Bruno, Grazia, Edda and Giampietro, Clive, Lucy, Alice and Holly. Last but not least are the majestic ibex, shy chamois and comical marmots, too numerous to name individually, who make this area so special.

## Updates to this Guide
While every effort is made by our authors to ensure the accuracy of guidebooks as they go to print, changes can occur during the lifetime of an edition. Any updates that we know of for this guide will be on the Cicerone website (www.cicerone.co.uk/923/updates), so please check before planning your trip. We also advise that you check information about such things as transport, accommodation and shops locally. Even rights of way can be altered over time. We are always grateful for information about any discrepancies between a guidebook and the facts on the ground, sent by email to updates@cicerone.co.uk or by post to Cicerone, Juniper House, Murley Moss, Oxenholme Road, Kendal LA9 7RL.

**Register your book:** To sign up to receive free updates, special offers and GPX files where available, register your book at www.cicerone.co.uk.

*Front cover:* Lovely Lago di Lauson is close to Rifugio Vittorio Sella (AV2 Stage 5 and Walk 4)

# CONTENTS

Map key ..................................................................................................6
Overview map.....................................................................................8–9

## Introduction..........................................................................................11
The Gran Paradiso National Park...........................................................11
Valleys and bases ..................................................................................16
Information ...........................................................................................17
Access ...................................................................................................18
When to go ...........................................................................................21
How to use this book............................................................................22
Path marking ........................................................................................23
Dos and don'ts .....................................................................................23
Emergencies .........................................................................................25
Mountaineering and guides .................................................................27
Maps .....................................................................................................28
Accommodation...................................................................................28
What to take.........................................................................................33
Wildlife .................................................................................................34
Vegetation ............................................................................................38
Local traditions ....................................................................................41
Further suggestions ..............................................................................41

## Alta Via 2 ............................................................................................43
Stage 1    Chardonney to Rifugio Dondena .......................................46
Stage 2    Rifugio Dondena to Rifugio Péradzà..................................49
Stage 3    Rifugio Péradzà to Cogne ..................................................52
Stage 4    Cogne to Rifugio Vittorio Sella...........................................56
Stage 5    Rifugio Vittorio Sella to Eaux Rousses ...............................59
Stage 6    Eaux Rousses to Rhêmes-Notre-Dame ...............................63
Stage 7    Rhêmes-Notre-Dame to Rifugio Chalet de l'Epée..............69
Stage 8    Rifugio Chalet de l'Epée to Planaval ..................................73
Stage 9    Planaval to La Haut ............................................................76
Stage 10  La Haut to La Thuile ...........................................................80
Stage 11  La Thuile to Rifugio Elisabetta Soldini ................................86
Stage 12  Rifugio Elisabetta Soldini to Courmayeur ..........................89

## Day Walks...........................................................................................96
1    The Lillaz Waterfalls .....................................................................97
2    Lago di Loie ................................................................................100
3    The Money Glacier Terrace .......................................................103

| | | |
|---|---|---|
| 4 | The Casolari dell'Herbetet Traverse | 108 |
| 5 | Punta Pousset – the local 'Gornergrat' | 113 |
| 6 | Beneath the Grivola | 116 |
| 7 | Passo d'Invergneux and the Mines Circuit | 121 |
| 8 | Laghi di Lussert | 127 |
| 9 | Pondel's Roman Bridge | 130 |
| 10 | The 2205m Mont Blanc | 133 |
| 11 | At the Foot of the Gran Paradiso | 136 |
| 12 | Over Gran Collet to Col del Nivolet | 141 |
| 13 | The King's Path in Valle delle Meyes | 146 |
| 14 | Vallon di Sort | 151 |
| 15 | Col Rosset | 155 |
| 16 | Punta Basei | 161 |
| 17 | Becca della Traversière | 165 |
| 18 | Legendary San Grato | 173 |
| 19 | Becca dei Quattro Denti | 177 |
| 20 | The Royal Track to Ceresole Reale | 180 |
| 21 | Sentiero Glaciologico Lago Serrù | 187 |
| 22 | Beneath the Tre Levanne | 189 |
| 23 | The Villages of Valle dell'Orco | 193 |
| 24 | Beyond the Dam in Vallone di Piantonetto | 196 |
| 25 | Nivolastro to Andorina | 199 |
| 26 | Frescoes and Fridges en route to Bivacco Davito | 202 |
| 27 | Sanctuary of San Besso | 207 |
| 28 | Col Larissa | 211 |

**Appendix A** Italian–English Glossary .......................... 217

**Appendix B** Route Summary Table .......................... 219

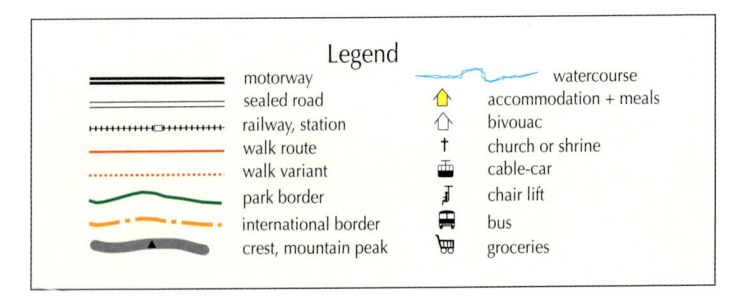

## Legend

- motorway
- sealed road
- railway, station
- walk route
- walk variant
- park border
- international border
- crest, mountain peak
- watercourse
- accommodation + meals
- bivouac
- church or shrine
- cable-car
- chair lift
- bus
- groceries

*From Col del Nivolet the Tre Levanne rise beyond Lago Agner and Serru (Walk 22)*

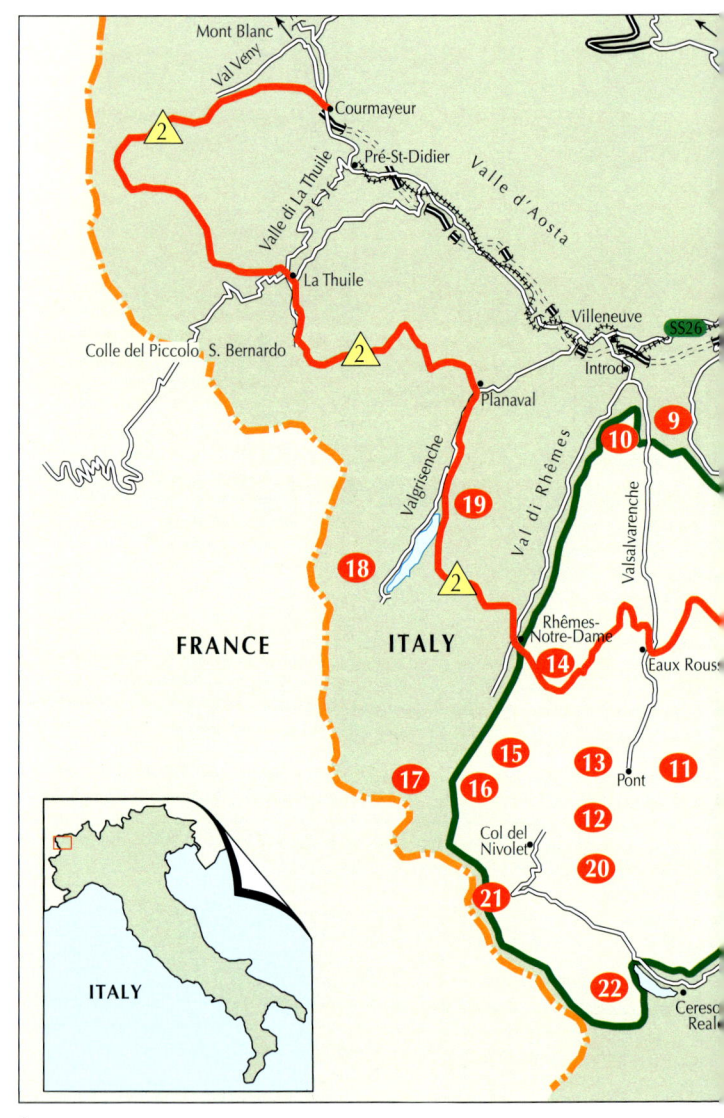

## *Gran Paradiso – Alta Via 2 Trek and Day Walks*

*Overview map*

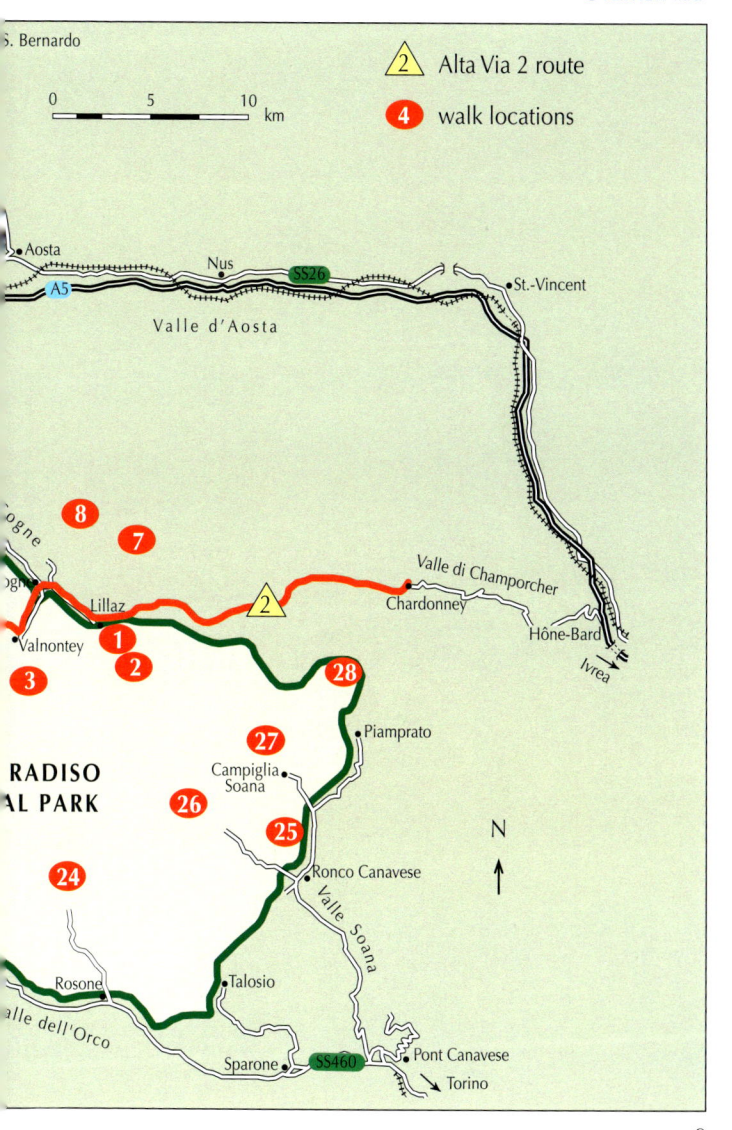

*Looking down onto Lac du Glacier (AV2 stage 10)*

# INTRODUCTION

## THE GRAN PARADISO NATIONAL PARK

*'Intending visitors to the district should be warned that when the King of Italy is hunting around Cogne (the present King has not been there since 1885) they may find their movements impeded by fear of disturbing the game. This will seem however but a small hindrance when set against the great facilities which the royal hunting paths (passable for horses) afford to travellers on the less interesting portions of many of the ascents in this group.'*

This introduction appeared a little over one hundred years ago in *The Mountains of Cogne*, one of the first guides to be published on the area. It was the work of alpine pioneers George Yeld and Reverend WAB Coolidge. In 1856 King Vittorio Emanuele II had unified several hunting grounds and declared a Royal Game Reserve. The move followed rulings in 1821 that prohibited hunting – except by royal entourages – in order to protect the ibex and chamois populations, which had fallen to worryingly low levels.

Ibex in particular had been hunted intensely since medieval times. They were considered to be 'walking pharmacies' as their blood, horns, bones and even their droppings were used in remedies for everything from poisoning to rheumatism. A special talisman was even made of the tiny cross-shaped bone found in its heart, believed to guard the wearer against violent death.

Not only did the ban on hunting encourage growth in both the ibex and chamois populations, it also guaranteed their survival as these were the only such populations in the Alps. After World War I, in 1922, Vittorio Emanuele III, grandson of the 'Hunter King', renounced his hunting rights and had the area declared Italy's very first national park 'for the purpose of protecting the fauna and flora, and preserving the special geological formations, as well as the beauty of the scenery'.

The Gran Paradiso sits in the Valle d'Aosta, in northwestern Italy, a marvellous region of magical mountains and rugged desolate valleys, verging on pristine wilderness. It is a mere alpine chough's flight from the Mont Blanc, Monte Rosa and Matterhorn ranges, landmark giants that can be seen from the many scenic passes and lookouts visited during this guide. Despite its attractions, the park is relatively undiscovered. Walkers can often enjoy unforgettable days on excellent trails through spectacular valleys that they have all to themselves, even at the height of the summer season.

*Ibex at rest below the Gran Paradiso*

The curious and romantic name Gran Paradiso goes back much further than the kings. While most experts say that the name Gran Paradiso, referring to the 4061m peak itself, is a contortion of 'granta parei' or 'great wall', some say that it comes from the presence of so many saints at the head of Valnontey – the peaks of San Pietro, San Andrea and Sant'Orso – and despite the nearby Punta dell'Inferno (Hell Point) and Testa della Tribolazione (Tribulation Peak).

## Walks and treks

In the mid-1800s around 350km of wide tracks were constructed at the king's expense, along with five hunting lodges and mountain huts, manned by a veritable army of gamekeepers (converted poachers), beaters and porters. A total of 470km signed paths are now on offer – a good few summers' walking! Altitudes range from a thousand metres above sea level to over 3000 metres in permanent snow. In between are strolls across flowered meadows and conifer woods, steep heart-testing climbs over rough unstable terrain (inevitably followed by knee-knocking descents) and even cool snowfield traverses.

There is plenty of variety and there are options for any legs or lungs. Do remember that the further you venture away from 'civilisation' and the valley floors, the wilder and more exciting the scenery becomes and the fewer two-legged visitors you are likely to meet. Rewarding holidays can be had by basing yourself at a comfortable village hotel or campsite and taking day walks out in different

## THE GRAN PARADISO NATIONAL PARK

directions. On the other hand, long-distance walkers with an adventurous bent can embark on the superb 12-day Alta Via 2 described at the beginning of the walk section. This traverses the southern side of the Valle d'Aosta over a sequence of forbidding crests and dizzy cols, connecting little-known Chardonney with the world-famous resort of Courmayeur, the gateway to Mont Blanc.

Otherwise, if you want to access higher altitudes and rugged landscapes, you can combine many of the 28 individual walks described in this book to make a longer trek. An excellent network of manned huts (*rifugi*) welcome walkers and provide tasty hot meals and sleeping quarters.

### Geography and geology

Geographically the area is part of the Graian Alps, the northern part of the western Alps. It was possibly named after the mythical Greek hero Ercole Graio (Hercules), who is believed to have passed through Colle del Piccolo San Bernardo while he was completing his famous 12 labours.

Geologically speaking the Gran Paradiso group started out over 230 million years ago as volcanic material, with a fraction of marine sediments. Tectonic activity led, in fits and starts, to the formation of the Alps during the Tertiary period (about 54 to 57 million years ago), the accompanying heat and pressure responsible for the transformation into metamorphic rock. The Gran Paradiso summit, for instance, is made up of a huge dome of augen-gneiss girdled by calcareous rock, mica-schists and greenstone, to mention a few.

Of great economic significance to man since pre-Roman times have

*View of Valgrisenche mountains during ascent to Col de la Crosatie (AV2 stage 9)*

been the immense mineral deposits, first and foremost the magnetite extracted at Cogne up until 1979 and processed at the Aosta steelworks. The original name of the Valle dell'Orco, the main southern valley, was 'Eva d'or' (water of gold) because of the precious minerals in its sands.

## A brief historical overview

The area covered in this guide, the Gran Paradiso National Park and its surroundings, straddles two administrative and political regions of Italy – the Valle d'Aosta in the north and Piemonte in the south (often referred to as Piedmont in English).

Historical highlights include the Roman era when the city of Augusta Praetoria, present-day Aosta, was founded in 25BC as an important alpine junction on the Via delle Gallie. The valley was controlled by the Savoys, almost without interruption, from the 11th century up until 1861, when Italy was unified.

Although French was the main language for most of this period and it is still taught and used, Italian is more widely spoken these days. Many local people, however, speak an unusual patois of French-Provençal origin. This includes a wealth of specialised vocabulary for aspects of the natural alpine surroundings connected with the pastoral activities, as persists in place names.

Demographically, the mid-1800s saw a significant growth in population which put a strain on natural resources. This led to seasonal emigration of itinerant tinkers, seed-sellers, chimney sweeps and glaziers from the southern valleys in particular. Later, however, large-scale emigration became permanent and ex-pat communities such as the one in Paris have actually helped preserve the Valle Soana dialect. Contact with home villages is kept up and French numberplates are commonplace in village car parks during the holiday period.

A 1981 census put the permanent population of the Gran Paradiso at 8359, in sharp contrast to the 1881 peak of 20,616. A large number of villages have been abandoned over this period and walkers will find themselves wandering along age-old paths punctuated with votive shrines and passing through long-empty hamlets decorated with intriguing religious frescoes. Higher up, the functional shepherds' huts give a clear picture of now-historic lifestyles.

Today, the Gran Paradiso National Park has a nucleus of 51 rangers (four of whom are women) who spend their time on patrols, carrying out essential wildlife censuses and discouraging poaching. The park does not have an easy life. Illegal hunting continues, storms frequently require urgent bridge and path maintenance work and, whatever government is in power, funds are cut drastically so that there are never enough staff or facilities.

## Some statistics

From its beginning with the royal donation of 2200 hectares, the park

## THE GRAN PARADISO NATIONAL PARK

*Vallon di Bardoney (Walk 2)*

today has a total area of 70,000 hectares (700km$^2$). Of this, 10 per cent is wooded, 16.5 per cent used for pasture and agriculture, 24 per cent uncultivated and 40 per cent classified sterile. A total of 57 glaciers of varying dimensions occupy 9.5 per cent. Visitors can observe a wide range of ice-related phenomena: vast rock slabs polished smooth by the passage of some ancient glacier; groups of 'roches moutonnées', so called due to their similarity to recumbent sheep; U-shaped valleys crafted by the long-gone ice mass and erratics or huge boulders carried far from their starting place by the glacier into different geological contexts.

The characteristic moraines, usually chaotic ridges of debris transported by the ice and deposited at its sides or front, are useful in determining the history of the area: bare moraine probably dates back to the last mini-ice age, a mere 300 years ago. On average, 5000 years must pass before such a ridge can be colonised by vegetation such as the pioneer mountain avens, after preparatory work by lichens. And trees such as larch or dwarf mountain pine need even longer (15,000 years in all) before the soil is suitable for them to take root.

Naturally the glaciers themselves provide abundant meltwater so the area is rich in water courses, spectacular waterfalls and dramatic strings of lakes of all shapes and colours. In the 1920s this abundance of water began to attract hydroelectric dam builders, who were given free rein on the southern flanks to provide Torino (Turin) with the power its industries needed. This led to a considerable number of large dams, conduits and power stations, accompanied by clusters of service buildings for maintenance staff.

## VALLEYS AND BASES

A number of long steep-sided valleys push their way towards the heart of the Gran Paradiso, providing fortuitous access for visitors. Nearly all the valleys are inhabited and have good tourist facilities in the shape of accommodation (hotels, camping grounds and high altitude mountain *rifugi* – see Accommodation) and tourist information offices. What's more, they can all be reached by public bus (see Local Transport). Beginning in the north and the Valle d'Aosta, minor **Valle di Champorcher** turns in west from Hône-Bard, gaining height to reach **Chardonney**, where Alta Via 2 sets out.

Forking south at Aymavilles, close to the regional capital of **Aosta**, the most important of the valleys is undeniably the **Vallon di Cogne** and its well-kept settlements. A pasture basin is home to the former mining centre of **Cogne**, while the sister villages of Lillaz, **Valnontey** and Gimillan are located a few kilometres away. Tiny Valnontey is arguably the best placed, not far from the Tribolazione glacier and its crown of beautiful peaks. Vallon di Cogne is a key transit point for the Alta Via 2 and the starting point for Walks 1 to 9.

Further west, from Villeneuve, **Valsavarenche** runs southwards as far as **Pont**, gateway to the Gran Paradiso mountain itself. With a decent choice of hotels and camping grounds, it makes an excellent base for Walks 11, 12, 13, 15 and 16. Alta Via 2 crosses the valley at **Eaux Rousses**, another fine place to stay.

Forking off from Valsavarenche at Introd is quieter **Val di Rhêmes**, the westernmost confine of the national park. Here the main settlement is **Rhêmes-Notre-Dame** (including the village of Bruil) which offers a full range of tourist facilities. Alta Via 2 crosses through here. Further up the valley a scattering of hamlets is dominated by the magnificent Granta Parei outcrop. Walks 10 and 14 to 17 can be followed from this valley.

**Valgrisenche** also leaves the Valle d'Aosta at Villeneuve and is populated with scattered farming hamlets such as **Planaval** (a staging point for Alta Via 2) and the main village called Valgrisenche. Glaciers occupy the valley head and Walks 17, 18 and 19 can be enjoyed here.

Two more worthwhile valleys are touched on in this northern Valle d'Aosta section. With its junction at Pré-St-Didier, life in **Valle di La Thuile** centres around the thriving winter ski resort of **La Thuile**. In summer it can serve as the departure point for the stage of Alta Via 2 which climbs to the magnificent Ruitor glacier.

Lastly we come to **Val Veny**, which turns SW soon after Courmayeur. It is the only valley with no permanent inhabitants, understandable in view of its location at the foot of the breathtaking spreads of glaciers that spill down from the Mont Blanc massif. The final stage of Alta Via 2 runs this way.

The southernmost Piemonte side of the Gran Paradiso has similarly good access and direct transport links with Torino. First to be encountered is narrow **Valle Soana** and the village of **Ronco Canavese**, probably the most suitable base for forays into the surrounding mountains, such as Walks 25 to 28.

The **Valle dell'Orco** winds its way west, with a fork at Rosone for **Vallone di Piantonetto** and Walk 24. Further along is the picturesque if diminutive village of **Noasca** for Walk 23. Soon we reach **Ceresole Reale** set on a lakeside, a well-served base for Walks 20 to 22. At the top of that valley, well above the dams is **Col del Nivolet** where the road ends. Here a couple of *rifugi* come in handy for Walks 12, 15, 16 and 20.

## INFORMATION

The head office of the Parco Nazionale del Gran Paradiso is in Torino (Turin) (Via della Rocca 47, 10123 Torino www.pngp.it). Visitor centres that hold exhibitions on local themes and offer guided walks can be found at Ceresole Reale, Noasca and Ronco Canavese in the southern Piemonte section and Cogne, Chavaney and Dégioz in the northern Valle d'Aosta section. The fascinating Alpine Botanical Garden at Valnontey also doubles as an information point.

Useful tourism offices are in:
**Aosta** Tel 0165 236627
  www.lovevda.it. This website covers all the villages on the Valle d'Aosta side of the Gran Paradiso park.
**Ceresole Reale** Tel 0124 953186
  www.turismoceresolereale.it
**Champorcher** Tel 0125 37134
  www.valledichamporcher.it
**Cogne** Tel 0165 74040
  www.cogne.org
**Courmayeur** Tel 0165 842060
  www.courmayeurmontblanc.it
**Dégioz** Tel 0165 905816
**Ivrea** Tel 0125 618131
  www.anfiteatromorenicoivrea.it
**La Thuile** Tel 0165 884179
  www.lathuile.it
**Locana** Tel 0124 83121
**Noasca** Tel 0124 901001
  www.comune.noasca.to.it
**Pont, Valsavarenche** Tel 0165 95304 (summer)
**Rhêmes Notre Dame** Tel 0165 936114
**Rhêmes Saint Georges** Tel 0165 907634
**Ronco Canavese** Tel 0124 817377 (summer) www.vallesoana.it
**Valgrisenche** Tel 0165 97193

**Valprato Soana** Tel 0124 812908 (summer) www.vallesoana.it

## ACCESS

### By air
The most convenient airport for this region is Torino's Caselle www.aeroportoditorino.it. It is well served by many companies from the UK and European countries. While the occasional coach does go direct to Aosta, regular city trains and buses convey passengers to the city centre and the main railway station, Torino Porta Nuova, for ongoing services.

Milano is also handy and has two airports www.sea-aeroportimilano.it, both well served by UK, European and international companies. Both Malpensa and Linate have direct trains to Milano Centrale station for links via Chivasso to the Valle d'Aosta or via Torino Porta Susa for the Pont Canavese railway – see below.

### By car
Drivers have a good choice of itineraries, which are also spectacular: from France via the Mont Blanc tunnel or the Piccolo San Bernardo pass; from Switzerland via the Gran San Bernardo pass and tunnel. From the south, as well as main SS26, the A5 *autostrada* (motorway) leads via Aosta to Courmayeur. For the southern section you'll need SS460 from Torino via Cuorgné and on to Pont Canavese.

*Comba des Usselettes and Rifugio Deffeyes (AV2 stage 10)*

## By coach and train
From the north, Valle d'Aosta can be approached by coach from France via Chamonix or from Switzerland via Martigny. Otherwise, you can arrive from the south by train via Ivrea as far as Aosta or Pré-St-Didier, only 5.5km short of Courmayeur. Long-distance coaches also run from Torino and Milano (Milan).

The southern flanks of the Park are accessible from Torino, which in turn has international train connections via Modane in France. From Torino take the train line as far as Pont Canavese.

## Local transport
Train information is available at www.trenitalia.com, tel 892021. Remember to stamp train tickets in one of the machines at the platform before you travel; failure to do so can result in a fine. The exception are tickets with a booked seat (showing date and time).

Timetables for all bus services in the Valle d'Aosta are available at www.regione.vda.it/trasporti, and local tourist offices can also provide timetables. In Aosta, you can get information at the central bus station (*autostazione*) (tel 0165 262027) across the road from the railway station.

When reading timetables or asking for information, you will need to know that *giornaliero* (abbreviated as GG) means daily, *scolastico* means during school term, *feriale* means Monday to Saturday, and *festivo* means Sunday or public holidays. *Sciopero* means strike.

The services are very reasonably priced and travel to even the smallest hamlet. In midsummer there are usually extended runs to points of visitor interest. Summer timetables take effect around mid-June, ending early in September, depending on school term dates.

The different bus company services are summarised below.

**GTT** Tel 800 019152 (tel 011 0672000 from a mobile phone) www.gtt.to.it has a direct Torino–Col del Nivolet return run on Sundays and public holidays as well as responsibility for the shuttle buses from Lago Serrù to Col del Nivolet on Sundays and public holidays, from early July through August, in conjunction with the Park's *'a piedi tra le nuvole'* initiative. They also run the train from Torino to the Pont Canavese railhead and ongoing buses in Valle dell'Orco and Valle Soana.

**SADEM** Tel 800 801600 (tel 011 3000611 from a mobile phone) www.sadem.it does Torino–Aosta runs as well as serving Torino's Caselle airport.

**SAVDA** Tel 800 170444 or 0165 367011 www.savda.it covers Cogne, Courmayeur, La Thuile, Valgrisenche, Val di Rhêmes and Valsavarenche.

For information on the local Cogne runs (to Valnontey, Lillaz and Gimillan) contact the Cogne Tourist Office (tel 0165 74040) www.cogne.org.

**VITA** Tel 0125 966546 for Valle di Champorcher www.vitagroup.it.

Between July and September the park runs a handy on-demand mini bus that links the Valle d'Aosta valleys. Tel 339 5443364 or 331 4950951 www.grand-paradis.it.

## WHEN TO GO

The park area and surroundings are naturally open all year, but access is subject to snow cover, avalanches and landslides which close paths and occasionally roads. The most suitable period for non-skiing visits is May to October. The high-altitude refuges function from late June to late September, although you can base yourself at any of the valley resorts at other times of the year. In May and June herds of ibex graze the fresh new grass on valley floors and even around roads and settlements, but by mid-summer they have returned to their rocky spurs and can be seen at about 2200m, never far from chamois.

For flower lovers, July is probably the best month. August is peak holiday time for Italians and valley accommodation for weekends is then best booked in advance. The higher refuge-to-refuge itineraries are feasible in high summer with less snow on the passes. Crowds are rare higher up although organised group tours are becoming more common on popular

*Lago Goletta (Walk 17)*

central routes. Late summer brings crystal clear days, burnt autumn colours and deserted paths. Italy stays on summer time until late October, meaning a bonus of extra daylight for visitors. The choice is yours.

## HOW TO USE THIS BOOK

This guide does not purport to cover the whole of the Gran Paradiso and southern Valle d'Aosta comprehensively. The itineraries explore highlights and special places to whet walking appetites. With a map and a sense of adventure, you will be able to concoct scores of other delightful walks.

We begin with the superb long-distance route, Alta Via 2. It lends itself to numerous variations and each stage could be followed as a day walk. The successive chapters of the guide contain walks suitable for visitors who prefer to make their base in a valley hotel or campsite and embark on shorter excursions. A handful of excellent traverses is also included, brilliant routes that convey walkers to wild exhilarating heights and act as links between the inhabited valleys. Suggestions are given for combining these into a further series of long-distance routes.

The descriptions of the individual walks and the stages on Alta Via 2 all begin with some basic information: time, distance, ascent/descent, grade and map required.

### Time
Based on a walker of average fitness, the estimate of walking time gives a rough idea of how long it will take to complete the route in good conditions. Roughly speaking, it is based on 1h for 300m of ascent or 500m of descent or 5km on level ground (but there isn't much of that). However, it *does not include* stops for rests or meals, so always allow plenty of extra time. Groups should always remember that their pace will be dictated by their slowest member.

### Distance and ascent/descent
Ascent/descent (or height gain and loss) is also provided, as is distance, although this is of limited usefulness in alpine circumstances. For instance, 1km might sound short, but combined with a height gain of 1000m, that works out at a 45° gradient, so you can be sure the path will be verging on vertical in places. Profile diagrams are also supplied for the Alta Via and include transport and accommodation information. They enable long-distance walkers to see timing, height gains and losses and the steepness involved at a glance.

### Grade
This is an indication of the difficulty of the route. Do remember that adverse weather conditions or snow cover will increase difficulty by several degrees.
**Grade 1** – a straightforward path with moderate slope, suitable for all walkers

## DOS AND DON'TS

**Grade 2** – a fairly strenuous alpine walk, but not especially difficult

**Grade 3** – some experience on alpine terrain is a prerequisite as there may be particularly steep and exposed sections. A head for heights and orientation skills may also come in useful. (Note: walkers with little alpine experience will be comforted to learn that difficult sections of popular paths are often fitted with chains or a length of cable attached to the rock face to facilitate passage.)

*Signboard Piemonte style*

### PATH MARKING

All the paths followed in this guide are numbered. This entails identifying markers carrying the number along the way, be they paint stripes on tree trunks and prominent stones or signposts at junctions. The style varies from red and white paint stripes with a number in black in the southern Piemonte region (in conformity with the Italian Alpine Club system used nationwide) to a system of yellow and black arrows and stripes in the northern areas covered by this guide,

*Path signposts in Valle d'Aosta*

namely the Valle d'Aosta region. The Alta Via 2 is distinguished by a black and yellow triangle and the number '2'. (A note of caution: the Forestry Authority in the Valle d'Aosta also uses red and white stripes for tree markings – do not be led astray!)

Then there are the lifesaving cairns, appropriately referred to in Italian as *ometti* or little men. These mounds of stones heaped up by thoughtful walkers seem banal but on an uncertain path in low cloud they stand out like beacons, while painted marks are swallowed up by the mist.

### DOS AND DON'TS

- Find time for some basic physical preparation prior to setting out on a walking holiday, as a reasonable state of fitness will make your excursions more enjoyable, not to mention safer.

*Alpe Gran Nomenon and Bivacco Gontier (Walk 6)*

- Read the walk description before setting out and start gradually, choosing walks suited to your experience and state of fitness. Start out as early as possible and always have extra time up your sleeve to allow for detours due to collapsed bridges, wrong turns and missing signposts.
- Don't overload your rucksack. Pop it on the bathroom scales at home before setting out – 10kg is the absolute maximum! Remember that drinking water and food will add weight each day. And as the afternoon wears on and that refuge never seems to get any closer, your pack will become inexplicably heavier.
- Never set out on a long route if the weather is uncertain. Areas such as those featuring extensive ice and snow fields can be unexpectedly submerged in a thick layer of mist, making orientation problematic. Rain, wind and snow are tiring and can make even easy paths dangerous. Do keep away from crests and any metal fixtures during an electrical storm and don't shelter under trees or rock overhangs. Ask at tourist offices or refuges for weather forecasts or check the local newspapers. An altimeter is a useful instrument – when a known altitude (such as that of the refuge) goes up, this means the atmospheric pressure has dropped and the weather could change for the worse.
- Tempting though it may often be, especially in descent, don't stray from the path during excursions, especially not to cut corners. This will cause irreparable

erosion and damages vegetation. Remember that your behaviour will encourage others to do the same.
- Carry all your rubbish back down to the valley where it can be disposed of correctly to save the park and refuge staff time and money. Even organic waste such as apple cores and orange peel is best not left lying around as it could upset the diet of animals and birds not used to such food.
- Be considerate when making a toilet stop. Keep away from watercourses, don't leave unsightly paper lying around and remember that abandoned huts and rock overhangs could serve as life-saving shelter for someone else!
- Wildlife should not be disturbed unnecessarily or handled. Under no circumstances are dogs allowed in the park, even on a leash. Collecting flowers, insects or minerals is strictly forbidden, as are fires and wild camping.
- Always carry extra protective clothing as well as energy foods for emergency situations. Remember that in normal circumstances the temperature drops an average of 6°C for every 1000 metres you climb.
- Learn the international call for help – see Emergenices. Don't rely on your mobile phone as there may not be any signal in remote valleys.

## EMERGENCIES

All walkers should have insurance cover. Those from the EU need a European Health Insurance Card (EHIC), which has replaced the old E111. Holders are entitled to free or subsidised emergency health treatment in Italy. UK residents can apply online at www.dh.gov.uk. Australia has a similar reciprocal agreement with Italy – see www.medicareaustralia.gov.au. All other nationalities need to take out suitable cover.

Travel insurance to cover an alpine walking holiday is also strongly recommended as costs for rescue can be hefty. There is usually a special policy for members of alpine clubs – see Accommodation.

'Help' is *aiuto* in Italian and 'I need help' is *Ho bisogno di aiuto (o bee-zon-yoh dee eye-yoo-toh)*. If you need help, experienced staff at refuges can always be relied on in emergencies.

The international rescue signals can come in handy: the call for help is **six** signals per minute. These can be visual (such as waving a handkerchief or flashing a torch) or audible (whistling or shouting). They are to be repeated after a one-minute pause. The answer is **three** visual or audible signals per minute, to be repeated after a one-minute pause. Anyone who sees or hears such a call for help must contact the nearest refuge or police station as quickly as possible.

The general emergency telephone number in Italy is 112, while calls for

*View upvalley from Rifugio Bezzi (Walk 17)*

## MOUNTAINEERING AND GUIDES

**Both arms raised**
- Help needed
- Land here
- YES (to pilot's questions)

**One arm raised diagonally, one arm down diagonally**
- Help not needed
- Do not land here
- NO (to pilot's questions)

*soccorso alpino* (mountain rescue) need to be made to 118.

The arm signals in the box above could be useful for communicating with a helicopter.

### MOUNTAINEERING AND GUIDES

Attractive rock and glacier itineraries abound in this region. One extremely popular route is the Gran Paradiso summit, its attraction augmented by the fact it is the one and only above-4000m peak wholly within Italian territory. A mixed rock and ice climb, it is best tackled with the assistance of a qualified local guide who can recommend further excursions suited to your experience and capabilities. Enquire at the refuges or contact the official guides associations listed below.

*Lago Lillet (Walk 20)*

## Northern valleys:
**Cogne** Tel 0165 74835
www.guidealpinecogne.it
**Pont Valsavarenche** Tel 0165 95304
www.espritmontagne.com
**Valgrisenche** Tel 329 0857865
www.guidevalgrisenche.com

## Southern valleys:
**Ivrea** Tel 0125 618131 www.4026.it

### MAPS

An excellent general road map is the 1:200,000 'Piemonte e Valle d'Aosta' map published by the Touring Club Italiano (TCI) and widely available both in Italy and overseas.

As far as walking maps go, Blu Edizioni has done a good 1:50,000 version of the whole park; its sole drawback is that it does not cover the start and latter half of the Alta Via 2 as they are beyond the park confines.

L'Escursionista (www.lescursionista.it) and IGC (www.istitutogeograficocentrale.it) both produce an excellent series of 1:25,000 walking maps. Appropriate maps are listed in the information boxes at the start of each stage or walk.

Most of the above are on sale at bookshops and newspaper kiosks throughout the Gran Paradiso National Park and the Valle d'Aosta, as well as overseas map outlets and outdoor gear shops.

**Note:** Due to the region's history, the spelling of place names varies considerably on both signposts and maps and discrepancies are common; for instance a col may be referred to as either *finestra* in the Italian version or *fenêtre* in French. Moreover the Valle d'Aosta Regional Authority is currently working on re-introducing toponyms for both maps and signposts in the ancient patois. In the not-too-distant future these may well substitute what are currently widely recognised versions in Italian and French and undoubtedly cause confusion. Be aware of this possibility and be prepared to exercise a little linguistic elasticity when map reading! Path numbering is also subject to ongoing revision and there may well be minor discrepancies between the path numbers given in this guide and those on new signposts.

The sketch maps aim to give an idea of the location of the routes described, together with significant geographical features, but are not intended as substitutes for the commercial maps listed above. They are intended to help with orientation and pre-trip preparation. (See the sketch map legend on page 6 for an explanation of the symbols used.) Finally, an Italian–English glossary is provided as an appendix; it contains a wealth of terminology found on maps.

### ACCOMMODATION

Everything from guesthouses, converted farms, cosy refuges, spartan sanctuaries and bivouac huts is available, not to mention campsites. Local

## Accommodation

options are listed in the individual walk descriptions. Whatever your accommodation, it is a good idea to settle your bill in the evening so as not to waste valuable time in the morning. *Affittacamere* is a B&B and an *albergo* is a hotel.

### Rifugi

A *rifugio* (*rifugi* is plural) is a manned mountain hut usually located in a scenic high altitude spot, providing hot meals and overnight accommodation during the summer. The majority are run by the Italian Alpine Club (Club Alpino Italiano or CAI) as well as local families and anyone is welcome to use the facilities. They come in a wide range of shapes and sizes, such as a converted hunting lodge, former electricity board building and an old farm.

The beauty of the refuge network is the flexibility it gives walkers and climbers. The atmosphere is generally friendly and helpful and the staff are a motley crew including students, assorted members of local families and alpine guides. They all share tasks, including unloading the precious supplies brought in by helicopter, jeep, mechanised cableway, horseback or even backpack. Due to the strict regulations, only refuges outside the park boundaries can use mechanised options.

As far as visitor facilities go, there may be a choice between a private room with fresh linen or a bunk bed

*Rifugio Savoia (Walk 15)*

*Rifugio Miserin and the sanctuary (AV2 Stage 2)*

in the *dormitorio* (dormitory) where blankets or a continental quilt are provided. A lightweight personal sleeping sheet (with or without a pillow case) is compulsory in CAI huts and recommended elsewhere. Likewise, a towel is essential as the majority of huts provide a *doccia calda* (hot shower). (You may need to ask for a *gettone* (token) to operate the shower and be warned that water flow is often timed.) In this book, all refuges have a hot shower unless mentioned otherwise.

CAI refuges offer discounted rates for its members and alpine clubs with reciprocal agreements. UK residents may wish to join the UK branch of the Austrian Alpine Club (http://aacuk.org.uk) if not the Italian Club (www.cai.it), both of which include rescue and emergency insurance cover.

Remember to change enough foreign currency before setting out on walks, as refuge staff cannot be expected to accept anything but euros in cash. Charges for bed and board were about €40-€50 a night at the time of writing, not including drinks. Credit cards are rarely accepted. Most large villages and towns have a cash point.

*Mezza pensione* or half board (meaning dinner, bed and breakfast) is commonly offered and usually an excellent deal. The huts all offer hot meals at both lunch and dinner. You may have the choice of a pasta dish or *minestrone* vegetable soup, followed by second courses of meat and various side dishes. Vegetarians will need to request special meals, which are not usually a problem and they will whip you up an omelette or cheese dish.

Regional culinary specialities may be on offer. Among those worth trying are: *polenta concia*, a delicious and filling thick cornmeal porridge mixed with cheese; delicate *carbonata*, meat stewed in red wine with spices; *risotto alla valdostana*, a rice dish with melted local cheeses such as fontina and toma. An interesting, if limited, array of wines comes from the few vineyards in the Valle d'Aosta, usually supplemented by the fuller-bodied (and less costly) Piemonte wines such as Barbera and Nebbiolo. Stronger stuff comes in the form of aromatic Genepì, known for its digestive properties and made from the flowers of the same name (and not to be confused with juniper). The *grolla*, a decorated covered wooden bowl with multiple mouthpieces, may appear after dinner – filled with a memorable mixture of coffee, red wine, grappa, sugar and lemon. It is passed around for measured sips and so called the 'cup of friendship'.

Local refuges with accommodation and guesthouses are listed alongside each walk description, complete with sleeping capacity and opening period. These dates will vary from year to year depending on local conditions, so, if in doubt, especially at the start or close of the season, do check by phoning the refuge itself or asking at the nearest tourist office. Generally speaking the summer season means mid-June to mid-September. Intrepid ski tourers will be pleased to know that many *rifugi* open in spring to accommodate them.

Summer advance bookings are only really necessary on July or August weekends and will only usually be held until 6pm. Should you change your route, do notify the refuge to cancel as expensive rescue operations (billed to you) might be set in motion when you don't show up. Guests should always sign the register and indicate their next destination (or tell hotel staff their planned route for the day) as it could help point rescuers in the right direction in a search.

In refuges, 'lights out' is 10pm–6am when the refuge generator is turned off, although breakfast may be served pre-dawn if the hut serves as a base for an important ascent. Walking boots, together with bulky ice and mountaineering gear, should be left on appropriate racks in the hallway and slippers are often provided. In line with Italian law, smoking is not allowed inside anywhere.

As well as the main premises, most refuges have a *ricovero invernale*, literally a 'winter shelter'. Spartan but always open, they are intended primarily for emergency use when the refuge is closed, although they could also be used by walkers out of season. Intending users will need to be fully equipped with sleeping bag, food, stove, utensils and so on. Water is usually available in the vicinity.

## Gran Paradiso – Alta Via 2 Trek and Day Walks

*Bivacco Davito (Walk 26)*

### Bivouac huts

A *bivacco* hut can be the classic mountaineer type, a rounded metal container (with basic bunk beds and blankets), or, at best, a converted shepherd's hut with running water, wood or gas stove and blankets. They are not always left open, thanks to inconsiderate users in the past. Information on where to collect the key can be found under the relevant walk. Please leave the premises in good condition. There is not usually any charge to use them, but a donation is always a good idea to go towards maintenance costs.

You will also come across a series of modest huts, 38 in all, marked on maps as Capanna or Casotto PNGP. They belong to the park for exclusive use by the rangers, and are not available to walkers.

### Camping

Wild camping is forbidden within the Gran Paradiso National Park, and allowed only outside its borders above 2500m. However, there are good facilities in most valleys and many camping grounds also have bungalows.

### Vallon di Cogne:

**Al Sole** (Lillaz) Tel 0165 74237 www.campingalsole.com, open year-round

**Gran Paradiso** (Valnontey) Tel 0165 749204 www.campeggiogranparadiso cogne.it, open June to Sept

**Lo Stambecco** (Valnontey) Tel 0165 74152

www.campinglostambecco.it, open May to Sept

**Les Salasses** (Lillaz) Tel 0165 74252, www.campingcogne.it, open year-round

32

## WHAT TO TAKE

**Valsavarenche:**
**Pont–Breuil** (Pont) Tel 0165 95458
www.campingpontbreuil.com,
open May to Sept
**Gran Paradiso** (Plan de la Presse)
Tel 0165 905801
www.campinggranparadiso.it,
open June to Sept
**Grivola** (Bien) Tel 0165 905743
www.campinghotelgrivola.com,
open April to Sept

**Val di Rhêmes:**
**Val di Rhêmes** (Rhêmes-Saint-Georges) Tel 0165 907648
www.campingvaldirhemes.com,
open May to Sept

**Valle dell'Orco:**
**Piccolo Paradiso** (Ceresole Reale)
Tel 0124 953235
www.campingpiccoloparadiso.it,
open April to Oct
**Villa** (Villa) Tel 346 5792146
www.campingvilla.it,
open April to Oct

**Valle de la Thuile:**
**Rutor** (Villaret) Tel 333 1372961
www.campingrutor.altervista.org,
open June to Sept

**Val Veny:**
**La Sorgente** (Peuterey)
Tel 389 9020772
www.campinglasorgente.net,
open summer
**Aiguille Noire** (Zerotta)
Tel 0165 869041
www.aiguillenoire.com, open summer
**Val Veny** (Cuignon)
Tel 0165 869073, open summer

## WHAT TO TAKE

The choice of gear to take can make or break a walking holiday. It is worth spending time beforehand on careful preparation. The following checklist may be helpful.

- Comfortable lightweight rucksack with waist straps; plastic bags or stuff bags to keep the contents organised
- Walking boots with ankle support and non-slip soles, preferably already worn in
- Light footwear such as sandals for the evenings
- Lightweight sleeping sheet or sleeping bag liner, essential for overnight stays in mountain huts (on sale in many CAI *rifugi*)
- Small towel and personal toiletries in small containers
- First aid kit and personal medicines
- Rainproof gear – either an anorak, overtrousers and rucksack cover or a large poncho. Walkers who wear spectacles will appreciate a folding umbrella, although it won't be much use in a high wind.
- Telescopic trekking poles to distribute rucksack weight over the body and off wonky knees will provide psychological support during steep descents and stream crossings, keep sheep dogs at bay

or even double as a washing line
- Sunglasses, hat, chapstick and high factor cream. For every 1000m you climb the intensity of the sun's UV rays increases by ten per cent. This, combined with lower levels of humidity and pollution which act as filters in other areas, and possible snow cover which reflects UV rays, means that you need a cream with a much higher protection factor than at sea level.
- Layers of clothing for dealing with everything from scorching sun to a snow storm: T-shirts and shorts, comfortable long trousers (*not* jeans), warm fleece and a windproof jacket, with woolly hat and gloves for emergencies. Gaiters come in handy for snow traverses.
- A supply of high energy food such as muesli bars and chocolate
- Maps, altimeter, compass and binoculars
- Camera, extra memory cards, battery recharger with adapter
- Whistle, small headlamp or torch with spare battieres, for calling for help
- Supply of euros in cash and credit card. ATMs can be found at most of the towns on the routes. Assume that a *rifugio* does not accept credit cards unless otherwise stated.
- Salt tablets or electrolyte powders to combat salt depletion caused by excessive sweating
- Water bottle
- Mobile phone, recharger and adapter

## WILDLIFE

### Animals

One of the main reasons for visiting the Gran Paradiso is the marvellous opportunity for observing wildlife at close quarters. To state the obvious, the best way to spot animals is actually to look for them – most are masters of disguise and perfectly camouflaged in their natural habitat. Desolate rock-strewn cirques may reveal fawn patches which, on closer inspection, turn out to be chamois. Levellish grassy ground is pitted with entrances to marmot burrows and abandoned farm buildings overgrown with nettles may be home to vipers. Uninviting rock crests are worth perusing with binoculars for the likelihood of ibex sentinels tracking the progress of walkers!

Naturally the formidable ibex, *Capra ibex*, is the recognised king of the Gran Paradiso. Also known as *bouquetin* or *steinbock*, this stocky wild goat is easily recognisable from a distance for its enormous backward-curving ribbed horns, which can grow almost to one metre in length on males, double that of the females. Well established and protected these days, they now number a record 5300, in contrast to the 300 reported by Yeld and Coolidge in 1893 and the 400 survivors after World War II. Males

*Male ibex grazing*

live between nine and eleven years and weigh on average 95 to 100kg. Females are smaller at around 65 to 70kg. It was the original Gran Paradiso stock that successfully repopulated the whole of alpine Europe.

For guaranteed ibex viewing, try the immediate surroundings of Rifugio Vittorio Sella in Valnontey. There on a typical late summer's evening the young males are silhouetted on high ridges clashing horns in mock battle in preparation for the December mating season. (In December it is anything but pretend with the females only on heat for 24 hours.) Meanwhile sedate older males graze unperturbed, ignoring onlookers, some distance from small herds of timid females with their young. High rocky terrain acts as a stage for their unbelievable acrobatic displays, although they shift around in search of grass and can even be seen on valley floors in spring. In midwinter the herds retreat to high altitudes, carefully choosing south-facing slopes to increase the chances of snow slipping downhill and revealing the vegetation they need to feed on.

Chamois, on the other hand, *Rupicapra rupicapra*, can also be seen in woods as well as the high rocky outcrops. Another type of mountain goat, the chamois is slender and daintier than the ibex, with shorter hooked horns and white patches on its face and rear. A recent count recorded 7700 chamois in the park. Their principal predators are foxes and eagles but long snowy winters take the greatest toll on both the ibex and the chamois populations. Walkers of either sex may be surprised to hear reticent lone males whistling at them to mark their territory.

It is hard to miss hearing the European alpine marmot (*Marmota marmota*) with its shrill whistle warning of imminent danger or seeing a

*Baby marmot*

well-padded rear scampering over grassy hillocks towards its burrow. These comical beaver-like vegetarians live in large underground colonies and 8000–10,000 were reported at the last count. Protected now, they were once hunted for their fat, used in ointments believed to be a cure for rheumatism. The belief was unfounded, however, and the practice seemingly arose from a linguistic misunderstanding: the real 'marmot oil' for treating aches and pains actually comes from the so-called marmot plum or Briançon apricot, whose yellow stones produced an oil helpful in extracting the active ingredients from rhododendron galls.

Red foxes may be of little interest to British visitors, but the easiest way to spot one of these pretty creatures is to wait outside a refuge at nightfall, as the scavengers come for titbits in the rubbish.

A sizeable carnivore currently returning gradually westward through the Alps is the mysterious lynx. Sightings of the tufted-ear feline with grey-brown mottled fur have already been reported by hunters and rangers in Valle d'Aosta, where it prefers the shelter of low altitude woods, the habitat of its favourite prey, the roe deer. (It is also known to hunt old ibex who are slower on their feet.)

Another recent but unwelcome arrival is the wild boar. Not a native here it was introduced to populate hunting reserves and has bred so successfully that it is becoming a nuisance, wreaking havoc in the chestnut woods. So numerous have they become in Valle Soana that the park rangers have to spend valuable time hunting them down.

There are also several amphibians to spot in the park. The common frog is renowned for its ability to spend winters frozen into ponds up to altitudes of 2500m, thawing back to life with the arrival of spring. On dry southern hillsides around 1500m the bright emerald sheen of the green lizard is hard to miss, while several varieties of snake are occasionally glimpsed, usually sunning themselves on paths or old stone walls. The most common is the poisonous and protected asp viper (no relation at all to the Egyptian cobra!). This greyish-brown snake has a clear diamond pattern along its back and is slightly smaller than the common viper found in Britain. It is always featured on the helpful posters in tourist offices, visitor centres and refuges. Extremely timid, it only attacks when threatened, so do give it time to slither away should you encounter one on the path.

Elementary precautions walkers can take are to keep their legs covered when traversing an overgrown zone, and tread heavily. Should someone be bitten, keep calm and seek medical help as soon as possible. Bandaging and immobilisation of the limb are usually recommended in the meantime. Remember that you do have about 30 hours' leeway, and if there is no swelling after two hours, it either means that no venom entered the bloodstream or that it wasn't a viper at all.

### Birds and insects

Higher up glide ubiquitous flocks of chaotic noisy orange-beaked crows,

*Chamois at pasture*

more correctly known as alpine choughs. Great chatty socialisers, they appear out of nowhere at strategic cols at the rustling of a plastic bag in the sure knowledge that they will be fed by walkers' crumbs. Their only equals in noise production are the raucous European jays, which flash blue feathers on their dashes through the mixed woods lower down.

Impressive shadows may be cast by golden eagles, who have a field day in spring and summer preying on young marmots and lambs, the scarcity of vegetation making it easy for them. The only competition in terms of territory comes from the largest bird in the Alps, the lammergeier or bearded vulture. Not a hunter itself, it prefers carcasses. It is able to swallow bones up to 30cm in length (digestion then requiring 24 hours!), and is renowned for its ability to crack bones by dropping them from a great height to get to the marrow. With a maximum wing span of three metres, its wedge-shaped tail distinguishes it from the eagle, whose tail is rounded when seen from below. The reintroduction of vultures born in captivity took off in 1986 in Austria and then spread to other parts of the Alps (1994 saw the first actual release in Italy) and sightings are now a frequent occurrence. Otherwise an impressive stuffed specimen is on display at the Chavaney (Val di Rhêmes) Park Visitor Centre.

Other fascinating spectacles are offered by brilliant clouds of butterflies which vie for supremacy in brightness – notably the metallic hues of the common blue Icarus butterfly which passing walkers cause to flutter up from their puddles. Perching on a thistle, you may also find the rare Red Apollo, pale grey-cream but with trademark black and red 'eyes' on its wings.

Last but not least, mention must be made of the so-called glacier flea, large numbers of which form widespread dark patches on the surface of glaciers and snow fields up to 3800m. It is one to two millimetres long, hairy or scaly, mottled brown and feeds on organic matter such as pollen carried up by the wind. Alternatively red-tinted snow may either mean sand from a far-off desert, incredible though it may seem, or cold-loving algae with a blood-red colouring.

## VEGETATION

An excellent place to begin admiring the remarkable array of alpine plants is the attractive 10,000m$^2$ Giardino Botanico Alpino 'Paradisia' in Valnontey, established in 1955 and named after the St Bruno lily *Paradisia liliastrum*. Over the summer 1000 labelled alpine species flourish there and of these a good 250 are found wild in the park.

The relatively limited woods are composed mainly of mixed conifer, dominated by larch and Arolla pine on the upper edge, along with juniper shrubs. Common are curious dwarf versions of trees such as the net-leaved willow and ice-age relict dwarf birch. Larch woods also share their habitat with alpenrose shrubs and their pretty pink blooms, as well as wine-red martagon lilies and the minute flowers produced by bilberry and cowberry plants, in preparation for their late-summer fruit.

The star of the park's flowers is the record-holding glacier crowfoot, which grows at heights of up to 4200m. Also at high altitudes, colonisers of screes and bare rock, such as lilac round-leaved penny-cress and sturdy saxifrage ('rock breaker') penetrate cracks and fragment the stone. Moving downwards a little, stunning carpets of white ranunculus and pasque flowers cover high pasture basins such as the Piano del Nivolet. Marshland is often punctuated with soft white cotton grass and tiny carnivorous butterworts, the blue-violet common variety or yellow-white alpine type. The famous edelweiss is relatively unusual due to a lack of the calcareous terrain it requires, but another ice-age relict, the delicate and rare twinflower, grows in several valleys on open grassland. Elegant orchids are widespread in meadows. The dark reddish-brown black vanilla variety has a surprisingly strong cocoa aroma close-up.

The alpine environment is extremely hostile to life in general and the season for high-altitude vegetation can be as short as 60 to 70 days, including growth and reproduction. Each species has developed survival techniques, ranging from thick hairy layers as protection from cold winds and evaporation (edelweiss), anti-freeze in its leaves (glacier crowfoot), as well as

*Edelweiss*

ground-hugging forms that minimise exposure, allow the plant to exploit the heat from the earth and ensure protective snow cover (cushions of rock jasmine). In addition to the beating they get from the elements, many also risk being nibbled by chamois (especially attracted to large-flowered leopard's-bane for its sugar content) and marmots (who go for forget-me-nots) and even thoughtless picking by humans.

Above: *Martagon lily*
Centre: *Round-leaved penny-cress on scree*
Below: *Purple orchid*

To end on a 'spiritual' note, a quick mention is in order for the insignificant-looking but strongly aromatic flower of the yellow genipi, found on stony grassland. Although it is rather rare and protected, local inhabitants are permitted to gather a limited number to prepare their beloved Genepì – a perfect after-dinner drink with guaranteed digestive properties to boot.

A recommended rucksack companion for flower lovers is the Cicerone pocket guide *Alpine Flowers* (2014), while Grey-Wilson and Blamey's *Alpine Flowers of Britain and Europe* (Harper Collins, 1995) is the perfect reference book at home.

## LOCAL TRADITIONS

It is worth mentioning the kaleidoscope of cultural events on offer in the region. In addition to the numerous castles in the main Valle d'Aosta, the most characteristic tourist attractions are the unusual 'Battailles des Reines'. Probably traceable back to prehistoric times, they involve two enormous pregnant cows engaged in (bloodless) battle, for the honour of being decorated 'Queen'. Each competitor has already established herself as best milker-cum-battler at the head of a herd. Emotional local tournaments involving entire villages start in March and the grand finale is the Regional Championship held late October in Aosta. Copies of the 'calendrier des combats' (open to all) are available from tourist offices. The practice is also extended to goats with the 'Bataille des Tzevres' held in Valgrisenche in September.

## FURTHER SUGGESTIONS

Otherwise long processions to high altitude sanctuaries are a favourite midsummer activity. Popular local events with a legendary or religious origin, they attract huge crowds, often emigrants who return every year for the occasion. Worthy of mention are the Notre Dame des Neiges procession to Lago Miserin (5 August), the mammoth San Besso celebrations at Campiglia Soana (19 August) and 'Lo Patron de Sen Grat' (5 September), which are all mentioned in the descriptions of the individual walks.

## FURTHER SUGGESTIONS

Walkers concluding the Alta Via 2 at Courmayeur will doubtless be extremely fit (if not utterly exhausted) and may like to proceed around the Mont Blanc massif on the popular TMB – see Kev Reynolds' *Tour of Mont Blanc* (Cicerone, 2015).

The mammoth Grande Traversata delle Alpi (GTA), the 46-day hike across Piemonte, also touches the Gran Paradiso and can be picked up in Valle dell'Orco or Soana – see *Through the Italian Alps* by Gillian Price (Cicerone, 2005).

*Leading up to Col Lauson (AV2 stage 5)*

# ALTA VIA 2

This exhilarating long-distance route cuts its strenuous way across the rugged southern flanks of the Valle d'Aosta, unimaginable worlds away from the busy traffic artery.

Heading due south from the main valley a succession of formidable ravine-like valleys gouged out by the impetuous passage of water lead between soaring ridges. They terminate abruptly, almost surprisingly in open pasture basins, havens of tranquillity and home to man and livestock alike. It is the task of the Alta Via 2 to traverse these high parallel barriers one by one. Originating just outside the eastern edge of the Gran Paradiso National Park, the AV2 offers 12 memorable, energy-packed days on a roller-coaster walk through the heart of the protected area, touching on well-established settlements in Vallon di Cogne, Valsavarenche and Val di Rhêmes, then on to Valgrisenche, Valle de la Thuile and Val Vény. It also offers views of some magnificent peaks – the Grivola, Herbetet and Ruitor for starters and the massive Gran Paradiso in the distance. Europe's sovereign Mont Blanc – Monte Bianco for the Italians – provides the breathtaking finale to the trek.

As if the AV2 needed any more to recommend it, the route is relatively untrodden, making for sublime solitary days after which all effort is amply rewarded with warming meals in well-run mountain huts and cosy village guesthouses. The 12 stages are split equally between high altitude huts and valley hotels to keep everyone happy. This also means that picnic supplies can be replenished at shops on a fairly regular basis. Only one day – Stage 9 – concludes at an unmanned hut, but a short extension to the route links in a comfortable B&B. For each stage, we have given a selection of accommodation in the villages but more options can be found on the websites of the relevant tourist offices (see 'Information' in the Introduction).

## Waymarking, maps and variants

The route is consistently marked with the symbol of a black-edged yellow triangle around the number '2'. The going is generally straightforward, suitable for almost every walker,

*Alta Via 2 waymarks*

## Gran Paradiso – Alta Via 2 Trek and Day Walks

although there is the odd stretch of unusually steep or exposed terrain rated Grade 3 (Stages 5, 7 and 9). Each stage would be suitable as an individual walk and could be easily be adapted for a day excursion.

You could also walk the AV2 in reverse, although that would mean – alas! – missing the thrill of the Mont Blanc conclusion. An approximate timing for walking in the opposite direction is given at the beginning of each stage description.

Two optional opening stages for the AV2 have now been added, doubling as a link with the wilder Alta Via 1 that crosses the northern reaches of the Valle d'Aosta. Starting out at Donnas, on the main valley floor, the way climbs via Crest (overnight stay at the dortoir, open May–Oct, tel 328 0514516, crestristorante@hotmail.com. Meals at the local restaurant a short walk away unless you self cater) to Champorcher. See www.lovevda.it and go to the Alta Via n. 2 page.

**Three-day extension:** If you have three more days to spare, an extension to the AV2 is warmly recommended to include an exploration of the spectacular snow- and ice-bound upper southernmost parts of Valsavarenche, Val di Rhêmes and Valgrisenche. Leave the official AV2 route at Eaux Rousses (at the end of Stage 5) for Pont (summer bus or 5km by road). Then follow Walk 12 to Pian del Nivolet

*Bridge crossing en route to Rifugio Vittorio Sella (AV2 stage 4)*

44

*Glorious Mont Blanc (AV stage 12)*

and on to Col Rosset and Rifugio Benevolo (Walk 15). After this, follow Walk 17 via Col Bassac Déré to Rifugio Bezzi and down towards Uselères, where there is a link to Rifugio Chalet de l'Epée to resume the AV2 at Stage 8.

**Getting to the start:** Coaches and slow Ivrea–Aosta trains stop at Hône-Bard in Valle d'Aosta. Year-round buses run up the Valle di Champorcher to Chardonney from the small square near the railway station, in the shadow of the fortress.

*Gran Paradiso – Alta Via 2 Trek and Day Walks*

## STAGE 1
*Chardonney to Rifugio Dondena*

| | |
|---|---|
| **Time** | 2h45 (opposite direction 2h) |
| **Distance** | 5.8km/3.6 miles |
| **Ascent** | 738m |
| **Difficulty** | Grade 1–2 |
| **Maps** | IGC sheet 3, 1:50,000 |

The Alta Via 2 begins amid the beautiful alpine landscapes of Valle di Champorcher. The close-knit local community, with its time-honoured traditions, is descended from herdsmen-settlers from Valle Soana to the south. Two picturesque stories account for the curious name Champorcher: the first concerns San Porciero, a Roman legionary and companion of San Besso (see Walk 27) said to have taken refuge in AD302 near Lago Miserin (Stage 2), where he was inspired to begin preaching. A second story attributes the origin of the name to the pigs once bred in the valley on the fruit

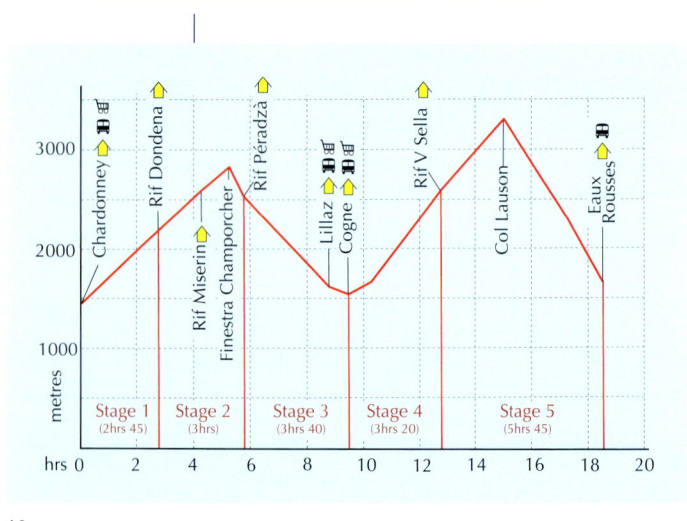

46

## STAGE 1 – CHARDONNEY TO RIFUGIO DONDENA

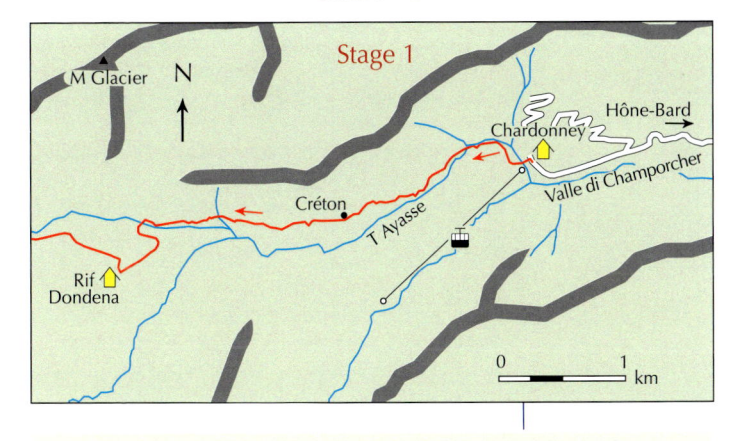

of the oak and beech trees that then died out after a dramatic temperature drop in the 16th and 17th centuries.

The starting point of Chardonney (nothing to do with the grape but a reference to 'agglomeration of thistles') has grocery shops where you can stock up on sargnun, a tasty cheese (object of the 'fêta d'i sargnun' village festival held late September) which comes fresh, salted or smoked. It is consumed with *pane nero*, the local rye-bread, these days likely to be freshly baked rather than rock hard according to tradition. It used to be baked only twice a year, leading to the invention of those wooden bread boards with a built-in chopper which you will see on display. A handful of hotels operate (such as Hotel Chardoney tel 0125 376011 www.hotel-chardoney.com).

Just outside the Gran Paradiso National Park, this initial stage entails a straightforward though steady climb on good paths, including a stretch of one of the king's old game tracks. Although rather short it does make a good introductory stage, especially appreciated after the rigours of travelling. It could easily be combined with Stage 2, either making an overnight stop at Rifugio Miserin or continuing all the way across Finestra di Champorcher to Rifugio Péradzà in just under 6h.

From **Chardonney (1454m)** and its cable-car, head uphill to the bridge left across Torrent Ayasse (AV2 signposting) and a stretch of royal game track amidst delicate laburnum trees. Not far up turn right on path n.9, a delightful old path that goes W through pine trees to Pont Ravire (1567m) and across the cascading stream. The path here is true to its name 'La Scaletta' or 'little staircase' as it climbs steeply on a series of rock slab steps.

A string of summer farms make good landmarks, including the cluster of buildings comprising **Creton (1852m)**, after which the traverse continues W. A further easy climb is rewarded by the lovely sight of Rosa dei Banchi and its snowfield SW, then the parking area and cluster of signposts where the track enters the lush flowered pasture basin of Dondena (2097m), well above the tree line now. The rough road proceeds past huts and old barracks to

**2h45 – Rifugio Dondena (2192m)** tel (mobile) 348 2664837, sleeps 80, open mid-June to mid-Sept www.rifugidellarosa.it. Although the concrete building bears no resemblance to the royal hunting lodge from which it was converted, all lack of atmosphere is amply compensated for by the hospitality and homestyle cooking, with luck including *polenta concia* corn meal porridge layered with melted butter and local cheese, along with a tasty roast, possibly rabbit. After-dinner strolls in the dark are best confined to the immediate vicinity of the refuge as this used to be a favourite meeting place for witches. In one episode a newborn baby was spirited away from its cot in the village of Donnas near Hône-Bard, but subsequently rescued by a peasant with the unlikely name of Napolion.

*Alpenrose and Rifugio Dondena*

## STAGE 2
### Rifugio Dondena to Rifugio Péradzà

| | |
|---|---|
| **Time** | 3h (opposite direction 2h30) |
| **Distance** | 7.8km/4.8 miles |
| **Ascent/descent** | 636m/298m |
| **Grade** | 2 |
| **Maps** | IGC sheet 3, 1:50,000 |

Well away from it all now, the AV2 leaves the summer pastures of the Champorcher valley following an age-old route that touches on the sanctuary of Miserin in its lakeside setting. A popular procession is held here every 5 August in honour of Madonna delle Nevi 'Our Lady of the Snows'. The cult originated in the late 4th century after an unseasonal (midsummer!) snowfall in Rome. Participants from the neighbouring valleys of Cogne and Soana trek over the mountains year-in year-out to join in a celebration of their shared history.

Next you face a stiff but unproblematic ascent, possibly across snow, to a broad strategic col, the Finestra di Champorcher which links that valley with the Vallon di Cogne and the edge of the national park. Once frequented by witches, medieval travellers, royal hunting parties, soldiers and herders moving their flocks, it was also used in the 20th century for the Superphenix power lines from the French nuclear power plant in the Isère. Fortunately, these do not detract from the enticing views over the vast spread of the snow-capped Gran Paradiso peaks.

From **Rifugio Dondena (2192m)** follow yellow and black waymarking W along the jeep-width track up the widening valley. Well above the tree line the landscape is brightened by spreads of flowers such as edelweiss, betraying the presence of limestone, and coloured rock such as greenstone. Overhead power lines and pylons are constant companions.

About 1h on, a marginally shorter variant to Finestra di Champorcher breaks off W, whereas left

*Gran Paradiso – Alta Via 2 Trek and Day Walks*

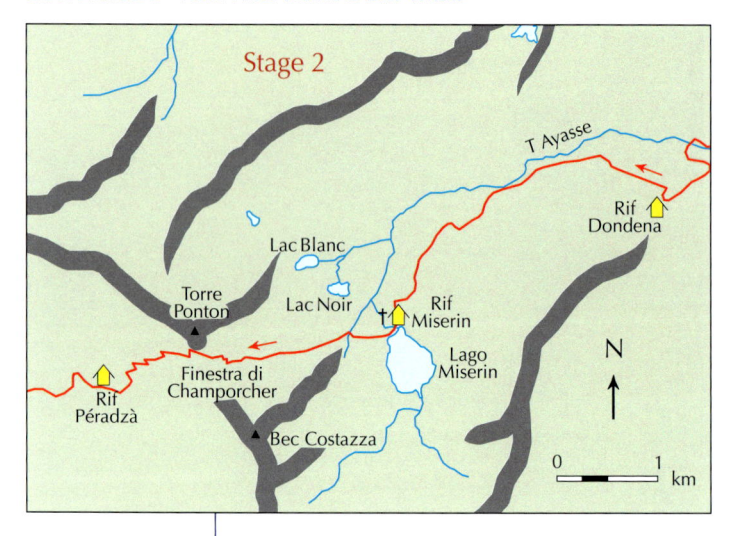

[Map: Stage 2 — showing Rif Péradzà, Torre Ponton, Finestra di Champorcher, Bec Costazza, Lac Blanc, Lac Noir, Rif Miserin, Lago Miserin, T Ayasse, Rif Dondena]

(SW) is the better-used track for Lago Miserin and the refuge. A clear path shortcuts wide curves, leading out onto undulating pastures and a glen housing the lake, sanctuary and

**1h30 – Rifugio Miserin (2582m)** tel 340 9014630 or 348 6813091, www.miserinespritlibre.it. Open mid-June to mid-Sept, sleeps 40. This spacious stone building was originally a hospice for travellers such as mine workers crossing from Champorcher to Cogne for employment. Adjacent is the unusually tall and asymmetric church-sanctuary **Madonna delle Nevi** which opens its doors on 5 August to throngs of the faithful. Both stand on the shores of lovely Lago Miserin, beneath the gentle contour of Rosa dei Banchi to the south, the most prominent if comparatively modest (3164m) peak hereabouts. (The name Rosa means 'glacier', whereas Banchi comes from a local word for 'white'.)

Cross the front end of the lake by the dam wall and take the clear path across rubble and any late-lying snow. In gradual ascent W it cuts up the left side of the main valley.

## Stage 2 – Rifugio Dondena to Rifugio Péradzà

*En route to Finestra di Champorcher*

Not far below the pass among masses of bright purple saxifrage you join the direct route, a continuation of the king's track. A stone hut, relic of a former military era, stands to the side of the pass but its precarious state makes it unsuitable for anything but emergency shelter.

**1h – Finestra di Champorcher (2828m)**, also referred to as Fenêtre and Colle, this broad pass opens up between Bec Costazza (SE) and Tour Ponton (N). Beneath the pylons are dry-stone walls for resting on and admiring the wide-ranging views, as you'll probably see ibex doing on higher rocks. NW is Punta Tersiva, the clear point of the Grivola stands out due W, Gran Paradiso WSW and the Torre del Gran Pietro SW, to mention a few. Yeld and Coolidge went to the bother of informing their readers that the pass 'was the scene of a skirmish, in September 1799, between the French and Austrian troops', at the time of Napoleon's Second Italian Campaign.

*Rifugio Sogno Péradzà*

Essentially heading W the clear path heads down the ample Vallon de Urtier in wide curves. The slopes are smothered with over-sized violets and the yellow flowers of creeping avens and pitted with marmot burrows. It is an easy descent past scattered evidence of small-scale mining activity to the brand new welcoming premises of

**30min – Rifugio Péradzà (2526m)** tel 0165 749111 or 348 6462534 www.rifugiosogno.it. Sleeps 75, open mid-June to mid-Oct, credit cards, hot showers, great traditional cooking, cosy rooms with duvets or a spacious dorm. The hut's full name is Sogno di Berdzè al Péradzà. Sogno was the name of former owners of this high altitude pasture. Berdze is the local dialect for shepherd or 'berger' in French, which also happens to be the current proprietor's name, while Péradzà is the peak due S, its small glacier feeding cascades.

## STAGE 3
*Rifugio Péradzà to Cogne*

| | |
|---|---|
| **Time** | 3h40 (opposite direction 4h40) |
| **Distance** | 14.8km/9.1 miles |
| **Descent** | 986m |
| **Grade** | 2 |
| **Maps** | ICG sheet 3, 1:50,000 or IGC sheet 101, 1:25,000 |

## STAGE 3 – RIFUGIO PÉRADZÀ TO COGNE

It is a long way down to the valley floor but getting there is enjoyable. Lacking the crowds of the park's central valleys the Vallon de Urtier has its fair share of chamois, not to mention romping marmots. A further striking feature is the stunning mass of wild flowers carpeting the upper valley in early summer. (According to the geologists, an unusual combination of calcium-rich mica-schists produced by the metamorphism of clay sediments alternated with calcareous layers is responsible for providing these favourable soil conditions.) Further down are light conifer woods. At the day's end is the friendly settlement of Cogne where a good range of creature comforts and transport are on offer.

From **Rifugio Péradzà (2526m)** a brief stretch of jeep track leads downhill to where the AV2 path resumes left (W). Marshy terrain hosts summertime concentrations of white ranunculus and pasque flowers, and several streams are crossed by bridges. (A link path crosses right to Broillot and other summer farms on the unsurfaced farm road at 2397m, a more direct if much less interesting alternative for Lillaz.) A brief climb is followed by a long, fairly level and especially scenic stretch high above the road. The steep mountainsides opposite were the site of intensive mining until the 1970s. Alpenrose and juniper shrubs, not to mention numerous black vanilla

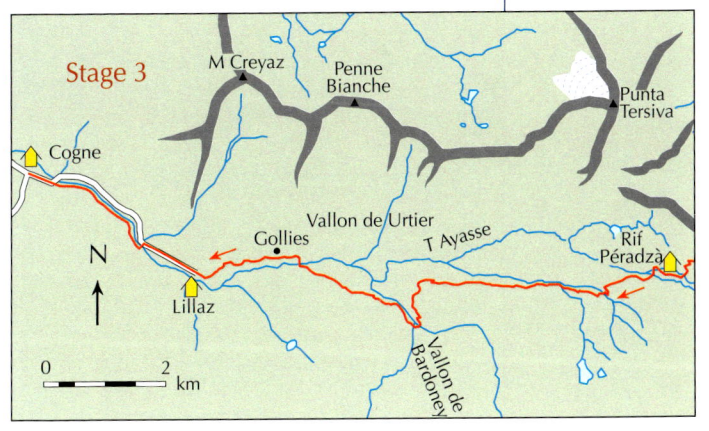

*Heading for Vallon di Bardoney*

orchids, precede a light wood of Arolla pine and larch – shade at last! The path eventually bears left (S) and yellow arrows point the winding way down past a park ranger's hut. Shortly you cross a bridge in

**1h20 – Vallon de Bardoney (2140m)** where the stream descends in a dramatic series of cascades and waterfalls. Here you turn right, joined by the path from Alpe Bardoney (see Walk 2). Zigzags through conifer wood lead to a clearing and intersection with a farm track. Close to Torrent Ayasse now, a wooden bridge is quickly reached and then you enter the tiny hamlet of **Gollies (1830m)**. With about half an hour to go, the valley narrows and immense slabs of glacially smoothed rock are passed above the Lillaz waterfalls (see Walk 1). Plastic water pipes accompany the path some way through pretty wood, catching up with it again down on the road at a small power plant. Then it is not far to the start of the road at the village of

*STAGE 3 – RIFUGIO PÉRADZÀ TO COGNE*

**1h40 – Lillaz (1617m).** Summer bus service to Cogne, limited groceries, accommodation at B&B Jeantet Abele tel 0165 749129 or Hotel Ondezana tel 0165 74248 www.hotelondezana.it.

*Flowered slopes in upper Vallon de Urtier*

*Gran Paradiso – Alta Via 2 Trek and Day Walks*

If you are not taking the bus, from the car park head down the road to Champlong where AV2 turns left over a bridge then down through pleasant woods flanking the torrent. The banal-looking shrine passed shortly is dated 1842 and bears the surprising painted announcement that the Bishop of Aosta conceded sinners a number of days' indulgence for every Ave Maria they recited there. The track finally joins the road to enter

**40min – Cogne (1540m).** This erstwhile mining and lace-making town has plenty of grocery shops, bakeries, an ATM, daily buses to Aosta as well as a helpful tourist office in the main square. In terms of accommodation, the choice includes budget Ostello La Mine tel 0165 74445 www.ostellocogne.it, Hotel Stambecco tel 0165 74068 www.hotelstambecco.net, Residence Pierrot tel 0176 749614 www.maisonpierrot.com or continue to Valnontey, below.

## STAGE 4

*Cogne to
Rifugio Vittorio Sella*

| | |
|---|---|
| **Time** | 3h20 (opposite direction 2h30) |
| **Distance** | 8.3km/5.1 miles |
| **Ascent** | 1050m |
| **Grade** | 1–2 |
| **Maps** | IGC sheet 3, 1:50,000 or IGC sheet 101, 1:25,000 |

Beginning with a pleasant stroll across flowered meadows, the trail touches on the tiny settlement of Valnontey, where a handful of hotels offer reasonable accommodation as an alternative to Cogne. This opening section can also be covered by midsummer bus if desired. Flower enthusiasts will enjoy a break at Valnontey to stroll around the attractive 10,000m² Giardino Botanico

## STAGE 4 – COGNE TO RIFUGIO VITTORIO SELLA

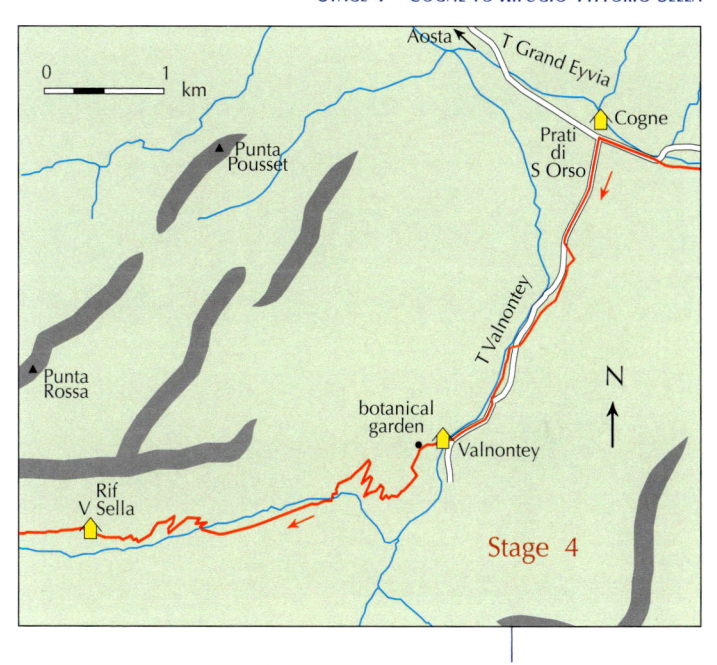

Alpino 'Paradisia' which boasts thousands of labelled species. Afterwards the trail climbs steadily on a former game track to one of the park's most popular refuges, in a vast valley above the tree line where wildlife can be observed all year round.

From **Cogne (1534m)** and its main square, AV2 follows the road SSW flanking manicured meadows – the Prati di Sant'Orso. They were named after Saint Ursus, an Irish monk believed to have freed the valley from poisonous serpents so the land could be cultivated in safety. A short way along go left onto a waymarked lane uphill through conifer wood. Further on is an underpass. Near a campsite you rejoin the road into

*Valnontey*

**50min – Valnontey** (1666m). Summer bus link with Cogne, small grocery shop, campsites. Affittacamere La Clicca tel 0165 74157, Hotel Herbetet tel 348 0345002 www.hotelherbetet.com.

Cross to the W side of Torrent Valnontey, where path n.18 climbs past the botanical garden towards a waterfall and up the mountainside on the wide easy curves of an old mule track. After larch wood, the last shade you'll enjoy today, the path crosses a timber bridge onto open terrain inhabited by marmots. You pass a series of summer farms, with views improving considerably towards the glaciers (S). Switching back over to the right side of the river, AV2 enters a vast basin. Soon after the old photogenic hunting lodge, now home to the park rangers, you come to the former stables which have been transformed into hospitable

**2h30 – Rifugio Vittorio Sella (2584m)** tel 0165 74310 CAI, sleeps 150, open Easter to end Sept www.rifugiosella.com. The hut was named after a highly acclaimed pioneer alpine photographer from the 1800s, whose black and

## STAGE 5 – RIFUGIO VITTORIO SELLA TO EAUX ROUSSES

*Walkers reach the old hunting lodge near Rifugio Vittorio Sella*

white masterpieces are unparalleled. Due W, tomorrow's goal, the notch of Col Lauson, is clearly visible. Make the effort to take an evening stroll S to nearby Lago Lauson to watch the ibex and chamois.

## STAGE 5
*Rifugio Vittorio Sella to Eaux Rousses*

| | |
|---|---|
| **Time** | 5h45 (opposite direction 6h30) |
| **Distance** | 16.2km/10 miles |
| **Ascent/descent** | 712m/1630m |
| **Grade** | 2–3 |
| **Maps** | IGC sheet 3, 1:50,000 or IGC sheet 101, 1:25,000 |

A magnificent, rewarding traverse and important segment of the trek, this leads to the highest point on the whole of the AV2, and highest non-glaciated pass accessible to walkers in the whole of the park, Col Lauson. Needless to say, a monumental knee-destroying descent follows. On the whole the landscape is surprisingly varied with both woods and vast grassed and debris-strewn flanks, not to mention sweeping breathtaking panoramas. Wildlife in all shapes and sizes is equally numerous on both sides of the pass, although on the desolate eastern flanks human beings are few and far between. The sole difficulty concerns the approach to Col Lauson: the terrain in its immediate vicinity is unstable and steep. In early summer the sheltered western side is inadvisable for inexperienced walkers as it tends to be snow-bound and may be icy, while by mid–late summer it is generally trouble-free and easily passable. Check at the refuge if in doubt. In any case, carry plenty of drinking water.

Leave **Rifugio Vittorio Sella (2584m)** on path n.18 and head W up the gentle grassed slopes of the wide valley. The gentle gradient and ample width are explained by the fact that it was another of the mid-19th century tracks that the king had constructed so the pass could be reached on horseback. After a stretch alongside the stream, ignore the turn-off right for Punta Rossa and

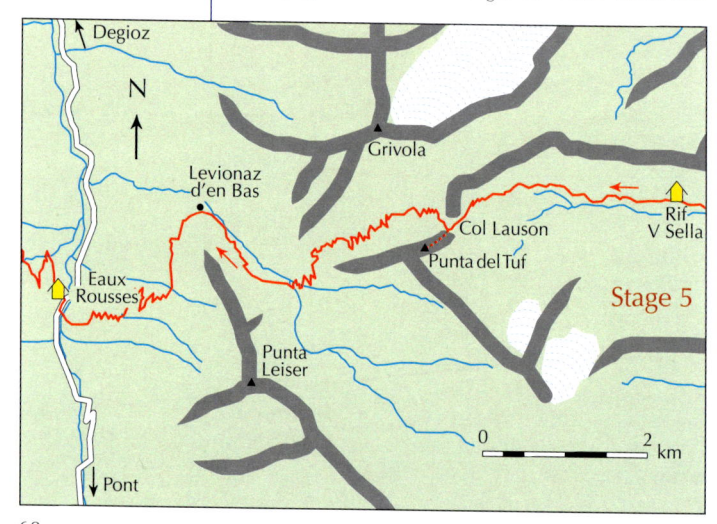

## STAGE 5 – RIFUGIO VITTORIO SELLA TO EAUX ROUSSES

continue into a final flat upper valley. The slopes are covered by debris, scattered with saxifrage and clumps of alpine buttercups. Ptarmigan are not unknown here and eagles inhabit the higher reaches.

In this lunar landscape the climb becomes decidedly stiffer and numerous zigzags cut up to a brief gully and a 'false' col (not the actual pass yet). This precedes a short exposed passage with reassuring cable, where a sure foot is essential on the crumbly terrain. It is then only a short diagonal climb away to

> **2h15 – Col Lauson (3299m)**, also called Col du Loson, which comes closer to the origin of the name 'lose', slippery black shale used locally for roofing slabs. For Yeld and Coolidge last century it was 'probably the highest path traversed by horses and not leading over a glacier in the Alps'. Views are partially limited here, although you can see the impressive Torre del Grande San Pietro SE back over Valnontey.

### Side trip to Punta del Tuf (30min return)

For walkers with some climbing experience, the ascent of adjoining 3393m Punta del Tuf is suggested for a greater panorama. In the absence of snow or ice, the peak can be reached in along the easy crest S. The view takes in Punta Basei (SW), Gran Sassière (WSW) and Monte Emilius, the Matterhorn and Monte Rosa (NE). The crest running SE from here to Gran Serra features an unusual series of bright to pale yellows, because of outcrops of gypsum-bearing limestones. The name Tuf is a reference to this calcareous rock, rather than volcanic origins.

The initial part of the descent, NNW at first, may be icy but by midsummer is usually clear and straightforward. This large, desolate valley is characterised by vast debris-strewn slopes which give way to meagre grass populated by chamois, ibex and marmots further down. A huge

*Heading for Col Lauson*

knoll (at approximately 3000m) affords a glimpse S of the Gran Paradiso peak, not to mention massive Mont Taou Blanc (SW) long visible on the opposite side of Valsavarenche. Dazzling horizontal strata of light-grey/brown-red rock, calcareous schist for the main part, characterise the opposite flank W, an outlier of the Grivola.

The path winds its way almost lazily downhill, in the wide curves suitable for the king's mounted hunting parties. Soon after a second prominent knoll (2700m) carpeted with tiny bright gentians, the path heads decisively but briefly S, and the craggy snowbound pyramid of the Herbetet (from 'small pasture') comes into sight SSE. After a bridge the path contours high above grazing flats with the ubiquitous marmots. Shrub vegetation including some alpenrose has begun to colonise the valley here and it is not far to

**2h15 – Levionaz d'en Bas (2303m)** or Livionaz-Desot, old farm buildings converted to park rangers' premises. Drinking water available. It stands on the very edge of an ex-glacial platform, with a dramatic plunge into Valsavarenche.

## STAGE 6 – EAUX ROUSSES TO RHÊMES-NOTRE-DAME

Heading SW the AV2 moves into the shade of a beautiful larch and Arolla pine wood. It is alive with squirrels and noisy speckled nutcrackers while the undergrowth is bright red with cowberry and bearberry shrubs. On a long level section the path seems to be unsure whether or not to descend until it crosses a watercourse. The final stretch is swept by winter avalanches, as demonstrated by a sizeable debris fan scattered with broken trees. At last a walled-in path through fields takes you over the bridge across the Torrente Savara to

**1h15 – Eaux Rousses (1666m)**, a cluster of old stone buildings including the carefully restored upmarket guesthouse Hostellerie du Paradis tel 0165 905972 www.hostellerieduparadis.it, which has an annexe-cum-dormitory for walkers. A more economical alternative is a short way down the road – Camping Grivola tel 0165 905743, open Apr to Sept www.campinghotelgrivola.com, has comfortable rooms and excellent meals. Year-round bus to Aosta. Nearest food shop 4km downhill at Degioz or 5km uphill at Pont. The name Eaux Rousses refers to the red rock behind the hamlet, stained by the water that trickles down from a spring containing iron ore.

**Note:** to extend the AV2 using the three-day extension outlined at the beginning of this section, leave the main route here and head for Pont on the summer bus.

## STAGE 6
*Eaux Rousses to
Rhêmes-Notre-Dame*

| | |
|---|---|
| **Time** | 6h40 (opposite direction 6h30) |
| **Distance** | 15.9km/9.8 miles |
| **Ascent/descent** | 1341m/1284m |
| **Grade** | 2 |
| **Maps** | IGC sheet 3, 1:50,000 or IGC sheet 102, 1:25,000 |

Another lengthy traverse with hefty ups and downs, this stage leads through fascinating landscapes with stunning views. Apart from welcoming Rifugio delle Marmotte, half an hour from the stage end, there are no intermediate refuges so you return to a valley for the following night's stay at Bruil, Rhêmes-Notre-Dame. The central section around Col di Entrelor is marvellous, despite the steep terrain especially on the northern side. Snow cover can be expected early summer, and possibly ice in the wake of bad weather. The wild broad valleys on both sides of the pass are well frequented by chamois and ibex, as well as marmots and foxes.

Both the initial and terminal sections of the itinerary would make good, easy day trips, suitable for families: Eaux Rousses – Orvieille – Lac Djouan and return, as well as the link with the King's Hunting Path in Valle delle Meyes (see Walk 12), and the Plan de la Feya – Vallon di Sort circuit (see Walk 14).

From the main road at **Eaux Rousses (1666m)** AV2 turns off the asphalt up through the narrow cluster of houses, and to the rear of the Hostellerie du Paradis. Close at hand is the trickling waterfall over the rust-coloured rock. A stiff climb NW for the most part, leads through abandoned terraces and into a dense and beautiful conifer wood mostly of spruce and larch and home to

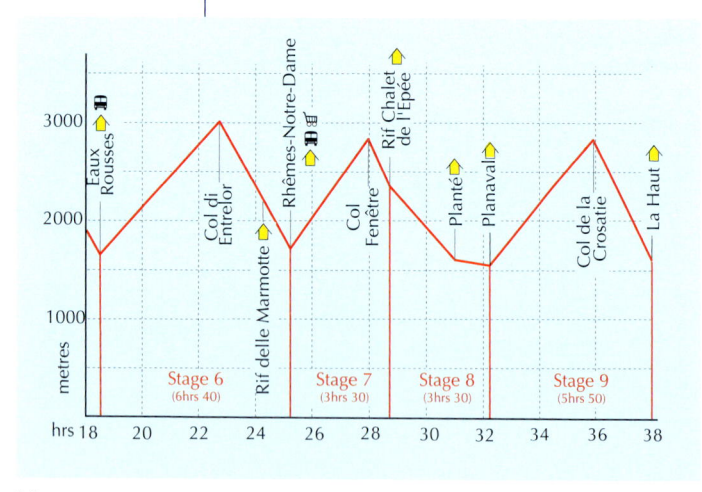

## STAGE 6 – EAUX ROUSSES TO RHÊMES-NOTRE-DAME

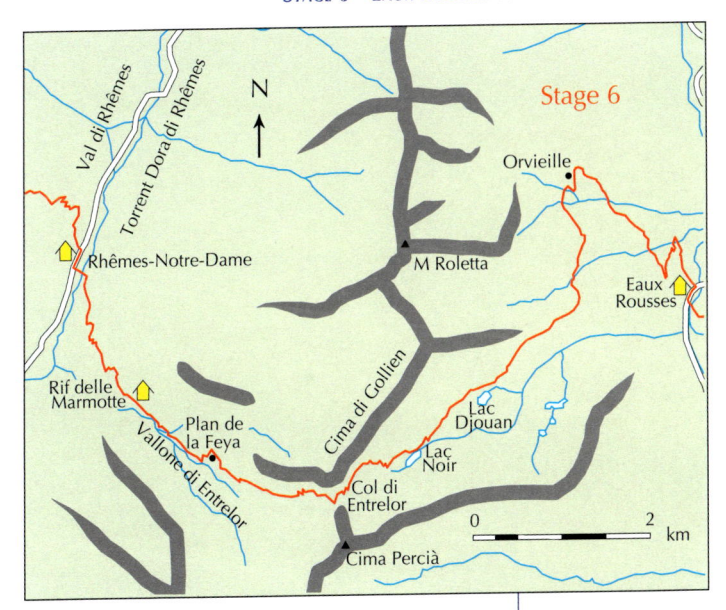

numerous squirrels and even lone chamois. As well as bilberries, the undergrowth includes the rare twinflower creeper, a delicate pink-white drooping bloom often found on moss cushions. The wood gives way to pasture and wide curves take you to the grassy flat of

> **1h30 – Orvieille (2164m)**, literally 'Old Alp'. The long building belongs to the park authorities nowadays, but it once hosted royal hunting parties and was a regular site for encampments, even boasting a telegraph line. Views here offer a good range of Valsavarenche peaks, as well as a glimpse of the imposing Gran Combin far away in the N, but the angle widens further with the ascent.

Heading S you follow the fence alongside the buildings where there is drinking water, then climb to a summer farm, where you'll probably have to pick your way through a muddy livestock feeding area. Several more

*Lac Djouan with Col Entrelor*

characteristic stone-roofed huts and wooden crosses are passed on dry grassy hillsides infested by carline thistles, crickets and marmots, with swallows overhead. As the trees are left behind, the outlook opens up onto the Gran

## STAGE 6 – EAUX ROUSSES TO RHÊMES-NOTRE-DAME

Paradiso (SE) and surrounding peaks, not to mention the elegant point of the Grivola (NE). Moving SW you gradually enter Vallone dei Laghi, its flanks bright red with bilberry shrubs in late summer above scattered golden larches. Col di Entrelor is now visible ahead. The path continues effortlessly to

> **1h10 – Lac Djouan (2515m)**, a peaceful shallow tarn, perfect picnic spot and worthwhile destination in itself. Apart from the alpine charr, a type of salmon, and wild ducks, this area is usually rewarding for herds of both chamois and ibex with their young – scan the nearby crests with your binoculars.

You skirt the N bank of the lake and soon reach a signposted path junction where the Valle delle Meyes link turns off left (S) and can be seen snaking its way up Costa le Manteau (see Walk 13).

The AV2 keeps right (SW) to a second lake. Despite its name, **Lac Noir (2650m)** is deep green and occupies a steep-sided basin where the silence is broken only by tiny, twittering ground-nesting birds. The path takes wide curves beneath Cime di Gollien (the name from local dialect means 'small body of water', a reference to the underlying lakes). Amidst hardy alpine cushion flowers such as saxifrage, it then narrows as the old game track peters out and a final stretch over loose debris leads to

> **1h30 – Col di Entrelor (3007m)**, 'between two alps'. From the airy pass, where a smattering of snow is not uncommon, you get a glimpse of Mont Blanc (distant NW), while nearby S is Cima Percià (pierced), then SW dark grey Becca Tsambellinaz, and beyond Punta Tsantelèynaz (easy summit) and its glacier in the distance, part of the border with France.

Accompanied by great numbers of white alpine mouse-ear, the path drops steeply W down rough terrain, snow-covered well into summer. It is both exposed and muddy, but you are soon back on a decent if narrow path with a more reasonable gradient into the immense and desolate Vallone di Entrelor. The small glacier beneath Cima di Entrelor (S) is responsible for the moraine which spills downwards forming long barriers. Ample grassy flats are soon reached with the promise of grazing chamois and romping marmots.

Stick to the right-hand side of the valley all the way to the curious vaulted huts of **Plan de la Feya (2403m)**, 'plain of the sheep'. Immense pointed Grande Rousse is straight ahead WNW. Here the AV2 turns decisively left (W) down a wider path towards the torrent. The first larch trees have appeared, and the path follows the right bank of the river to another flowered pasture flat and a knoll (Entrelor, 2143m) with **Rifugio delle Marmotte**. Tel 389 3488785, sleeps 12, open mid-June to mid-Sept www.rifugiodellemarmotte.it. The beautifully renovated buildings are set on the lip of Val di Rhêmes.

A delightful wander goes NW through larch wood, golden in late summer with brilliant russet undergrowth, but bilberries for earlier walkers. The path descends in easy zigzags, past an excellent lookout to the unmistakable majestic light limestone form of the Granta Parei SSW at the head of the valley. Diagonally beneath the

*Bruil, Rhêmes-Notre-Dame*

## STAGE 7 – RHÊMES-NOTRE-DAME TO RIFUGIO CHALET DE L'EPÉE

prominent rock dubbed Castel di Cucco, the path eventually exits on the valley floor, where only a bridge separates you from the peaceful village of

> **2h30 – Bruil, Rhêmes-Notre-Dame (1723m)**. The village boasts shops and a year-round bus service to Aosta, not to mention a delightful 18th-century church where a sundial reminds passers-by that 'Nos jours passent comme l'ombre' ('Our days pass by like shade'). Chez Lydia tel 0165 936103 www.hotelchezlidia.it or Agriturismo Lo Sabot tel 0165 936150. At nearby Chavaney is a National Park Visitor Centre with an astounding stuffed lammergeier or bearded vulture, one of the valley's last specimens from the times when the locals were paid to shoot them. (Note: Rhêmes-Notre-Dame is used to refer to the grouping of villages in upper Val di Rhêmes. Bruil is the principal settlement.)

## STAGE 7
*Rhêmes-Notre-Dame to Rifugio Chalet de l'Epée*

| | |
|---|---|
| Time | 3h30 (opposite direction 2h30) |
| Distance | 7.4km/4.5 miles |
| Ascent/descent | 1117m/470m |
| Grade | 2–3 |
| Maps | IGC sheet 3, 1:50,000 or L'Escursionista sheet 3, 1:25,000 |

Another worthwhile traverse linking lovely Val di Rhêmes with quiet rural Valgrisenche, where accommodation and homely meals are provided by the hospitable local family that run the *rifugio*. The AV2 leaves the national park from here on, but wildlife is still plentiful. (They can't read the signs.) A good path crosses Col Fenêtre; however, snow and ice on the steep eastern side immediately below the pass could be tricky at the very start of the season and it involves a rather long and monotonous 1117m ascent. On the other hand, this is a fairly short day's walking.

*Gran Paradiso – Alta Via 2 Trek and Day Walks*

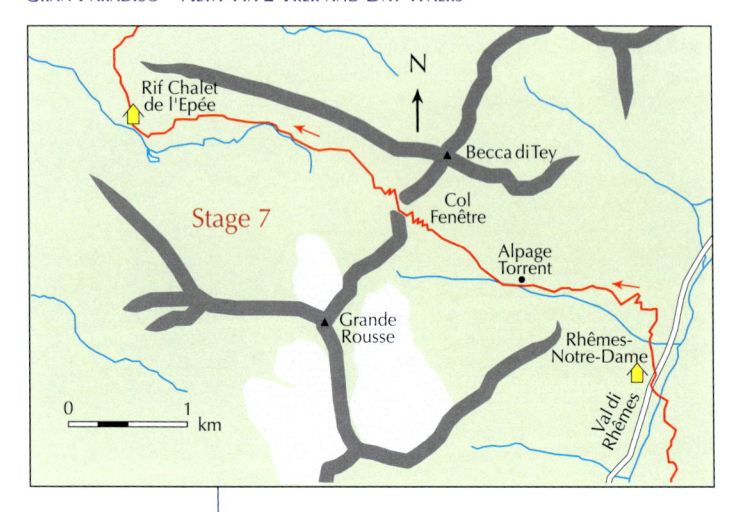

From the centre of **Bruil, Rhêmes-Notre-Dame (1723m)** the AV2 follows the road for a short way N, branching off left at a car park and across meadows. Needless to say it is not long before the climb begins, and you cross a torrent a couple of times. Soon heading W, the route goes through larch and past a prominent outcrop. The clear path traverses steep dry hillsides enlivened by hosts of butterflies such as the red Apollo, common blue and the smaller red and black burnet moth. Unusual stone huts with broad roofing slabs are encountered at **Alpage Torrent (2179m)**, all but blending into the boulders that act as their walls. Tight zigzags climb through densely flowered marmot territory towards rubble-strewn slopes, as the gradient becomes steeper and the terrain more laborious and the grass is left behind. Depending on the state of the path, it may be necessary to clamber the final tiring metres to

**2h45 – Col Fenêtre (2840m).** This scenic spot includes views to Gran Becca du Mont (WNW), Testa del Ruitor (NW) with Mont Blanc and its group

*Stage 7 – Rhêmes-Notre-Dame to Rifugio Chalet de l'Epée*

*Alpage Torrent*

*Gran Paradiso – Alta Via 2 Trek and Day Walks*

beyond and, looking E, Gran Paradiso (SE) and the village of Bruil some giddy 1100m below on the valley floor. More often than not the pass is occupied by ibex, so approach with care as they unfailingly dislodge loose stones if spurred to sudden flight.

The gradient is gentler now and the path curves right across a rock and earth mix, bearing generally W in the shade of a vast brown ridge culminating in Becca di Tey (NE). The opposite side of the valley consists of light grey scree spills from graceful rock flanks, outrunners of Grande Rousse and home to eagles. Following a stream, you drop into an idyllic emerald green pasture basin inhabited by noisy flocks of yellow-beaked alpine choughs. Further down a livestock track is joined to

**45min – Rifugio Chalet de l'Epée (2370m)** tel 0165 97215, sleeps 80, open weekends Mar to June, then 15 June to 20 Sept www.rifugioepee.com. The outlook ranges over the western flanks of Valgrisenche, where the prominent Ruitor peak stands out and you can glimpse its glacier. The original building, a shepherd's hut, which can be seen in the photo in the restaurant, was called Chalet l'Epère, from 'pierres', stones, due to the rocky nature of the surrounding terrain. A comfortable stay is guaranteed in this family-run chalet, opened in summer 1968. Meal suggestions include polenta (corn meal) mixed with fontina cheese and butter from the nearby farm, as well as home-made sausages and stews such as carbonata, in addition to delicious bilberries served with fresh cream. A fitting conclusion is a miniature glass of grappa (spirit) flavoured with local aromatic herbs or fruit from the custodian's collection.

## STAGE 8
*Rifugio Chalet de l'Epée to Planaval*

| | |
|---|---|
| Time | 3h30 (opposite direction 4h30) |
| Distance | 13.4km/8.3 miles |
| Ascent/descent | 148m/934m |
| Grade | 2 |
| Map | L'Escursionista sheet 3, 1:25,000 |

This easy stage drops across medium altitude pasture with masses of wildflowers, as well as views towards the Testa del Ruitor and its entourage of glaciers. Down on the floor of rural Valgrisenche AV2 alternates farm tracks with short bits of tarmac. Groceries and ATM are available at the main village of Valgrisenche, where there's also a bus. Your destination is a tiny hamlet with a comfortable hotel geared to walkers' needs.

**Note:** This stage is a good chance to rest ahead of the demanding stage tomorrow.

Bid farewell to **Rifugio Chalet de l'Epée (2370m)** and take the clear path (AV2 and n.9) NNW contouring across slopes with pretty shrubs, bilberries and martagon lilies, not to mention marmots. A slow descent winds down to a farm track (**Praz-Londzet, 2184m**) where you go right (NW). Steady descent leads through pasture to a path in woodland due N.

Afterwards you pass close to the football stadium. Over a bridge is the hamlet of Mondanges where you follow the road down to the village of **Valgrisenche (1664m)**; year-round buses to Aosta, groceries. Follow the signposts and waymarks to cross the river and continue N via a series of hamlets and vegetable gardens to Chez Carral (Maison des Myrtilles tel 0165 97118).

Walk straight on to the cluster of houses at La Frassy and soon break off left to Prariond (1549m), which boasts a curious monastery-like building on the roadside,

## GRAN PARADISO – ALTA VIA 2 TREK AND DAY WALKS

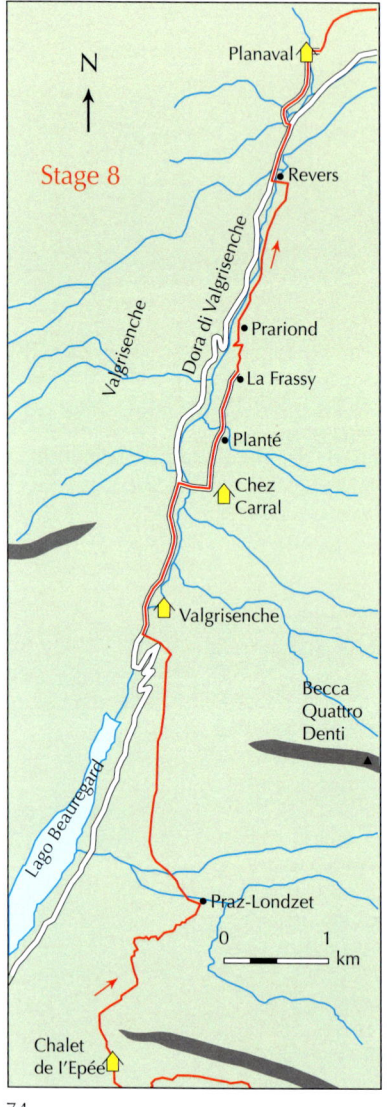

which turns out to be a historic stable and hayloft!

Without crossing the torrent, the AV2 takes a series of quiet lanes right (N) to **Revers (1530m)** and a deliciously cool drinking fountain. The dramatic gorge of the Dora di Valgrisenche torrent is finally crossed here. Follow the main road right briefly for the fork to

> **1h10 – Planaval (1554m)**. Hotel Paramount tel 0165 97106, credit cards www.paramonthotelristorante.com. Remember to settle your bill in the evening and request early breakfast if you aim for a head start in the morning. This modest farming village is set at the foot of sheer cliffs and a crashing waterfall.

**Note:** Needs be, it is possible to skip the long stages ahead and catch a bus from Planaval down to the main Aosta valley then on to La Thuile to pick up Stage 11.

*Stage 8 – Rifugio Chalet de l'Epée to Planaval*

*The hotel at Planaval*

## STAGE 9
### Planaval to La Haut

| | |
|---|---|
| **Time** | 5h50 (opposite direction 5h30) |
| **Distance** | 11km/6.8 miles |
| **Ascent/descent** | 1284m/1189m |
| **Grade** | 2–3 |
| **Map** | L'Escursionista sheet 2, 1:25,000 |

This is a very long day but guarantees plenty of rewards in the form of beautiful wild valleys, very few other walkers and spectacular views from the

*Leaving Planaval*

## STAGE 9 – PLANAVAL TO LA HAUT

pass. The AV2 used to cross the glacier via Colle de Planaval, but has now been rerouted. Although this has added an extra day, it has made the route accessible to all walkers. Accommodation is at a friendly agriturismo, whose owners will pick you up at La Haut, drive you down to Lazey for a delicious dinner and overnight stay, and bring you back the next morning.

**Note:** Weather and energy permitting, it is feasible to avoid the descent to La Haut and press on to Rifugio Deffeyes – a total of 8hr 25min.

From the hotel at **Planaval (1554m)** continue through the pretty farming village past the church and across the torrent. Keep to the left fork towards the hamlet of **La Clusaz**, where the tarmac veers left below the houses. A batch of signposts soon point AV2 walkers to the start of the path, which begins its climb WNW through shady

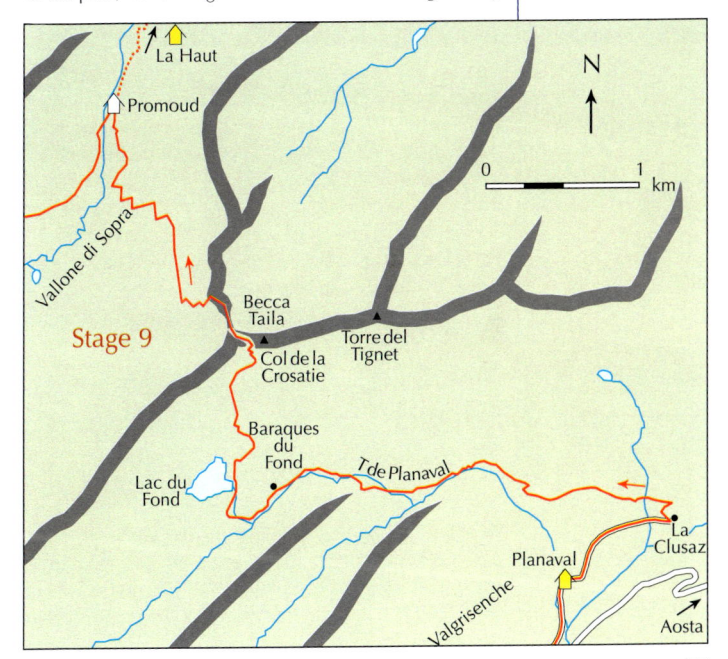

*On the way to Baraques du Fond in the company of Testa del Ruitor*

mixed woodland. With constant zigzags on the right bank of the Torrent de Planaval and improving views over Valgrisenche, it reaches flower-covered mountainsides thick with crickets. The gradient eases temporarily as you enter an attractive valley with a meandering stream and marshes prickly with cotton grass and purple orchids. Ahead SW rises the Testa del Ruitor and its spreading glacier – quite a sight!

Slabs of glacially smoothed rock accompany you to a further terrace and

**2h10 – Baraques du Fond (2340m)**, a collection of picturesque abandoned huts.

Here the AV2 parts ways with the direct glacier crossing over Colle de Planaval to Rifugio Deffeyes, the former route. Turning off right, initially W, it ascends to **Lac du Fond (2439m)**, a tiny tarn nestling in a deep, cup-shaped depression.

## STAGE 9 – PLANAVAL TO LA HAUT

The path embarks on a perfectly graded ascent N, with steps occasionally cut into the rock face but no exposure to speak of. Scattered flowers and noisy crickets are still present. Enjoy the final views of Valgrisenche as you leave them behind for

*Lac du Fond with the Ruitor*

> **1h30 – Col de la Crosatie (2838m)**. Take a breath and drink in the superbly magnificent line-up of the Mont Blanc range. Closer at hand Vallone di Sopra with Promoud is directly at your feet, while right of the pass is a dark dizzy rock point, Becca Taila, where the local goats play precarious hanging-on games.

A clear path plunges downhill NNW, with good solid steps traversing a massive stone-ridden slope. A couple of hundred metres lower down things become greener and alpenrose shrubs appear, in bloom if you are lucky. Grass and the shade of trees are finally gained. The path as such disappears momentarily and you need to follow yellow arrows carefully towards the watercourse. Across the bridge is

*Waymarking on the Col de la Crosatie*

**1h30 – Promoud (2022m)**. Unfortunately, the bivouac hut here was swept away by an avalanche.

Now point your boots N on the clear path (n.100) to the right of the stream. It descends easily through beautiful woodland, emerging at a lane.

**40min – La Haut (1649m)** tel 0165 861091 or 348 1651665, alexrampin71@yahoo.it c/o Agriturismo La Roueige, Lazey. Sleeps 4.

## STAGE 10
*La Haut to La Thuile*

| | |
|---|---|
| Time | 7h15 (opposite direction 7h40) |
| Distance | 16km/10 miles |
| Ascent/descent | 1211m/1425m |
| Grade | 2 |
| Map | L'Escursionista sheet 2, 1:25,000 |

## STAGE 10 – LA HAUT TO LA THUILE

An extremely varied and very long day concluding with a knee-weakening descent. It sets out from an isolated valley with only a handful of shepherds and livestock, then traverses over a panoramic col to descend a justifiably popular valley punctuated with a wealth of spectacular waterfalls. The stage concludes at the town of La Thuile, with all supplies and services.

Walkers with plenty of time on their hands are advised to shorten the stage by staying overnight at the scenically positioned Rifugio Deffeyes. This will allow time for a side trip towards the glacier, as well as a leisurely descent to La Thuile the following day.

Leave **La Haut (1649m)** and return uphill on path n.100 in the company of a stream, all the way through wood to **Promoud (2022m)**. Immediately uphill from the farm buildings, the AV2 begins its climb SW through a larch wood with alpenrose and a thick carpet of bilberries, high above a meandering stream. As the wood gives out, stony slopes take over, the result of old rockfalls beneath M. Mochet. A series of cirques follows with possible snow patches, but waymarking is constant. The gradient gets

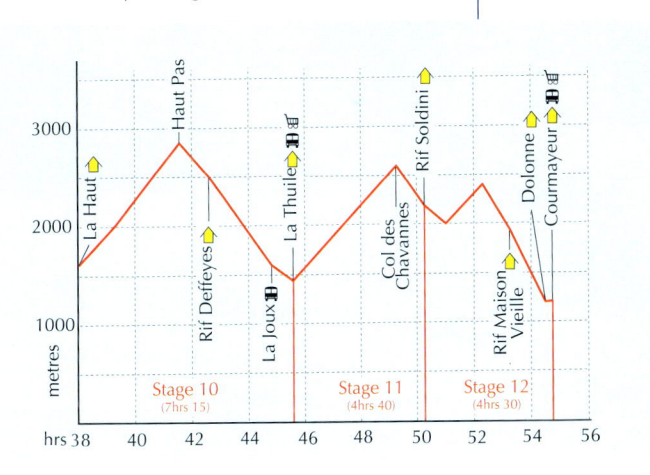

*Late-lying snow before Haut Pas*

## STAGE 10 – LA HAUT TO LA THUILE

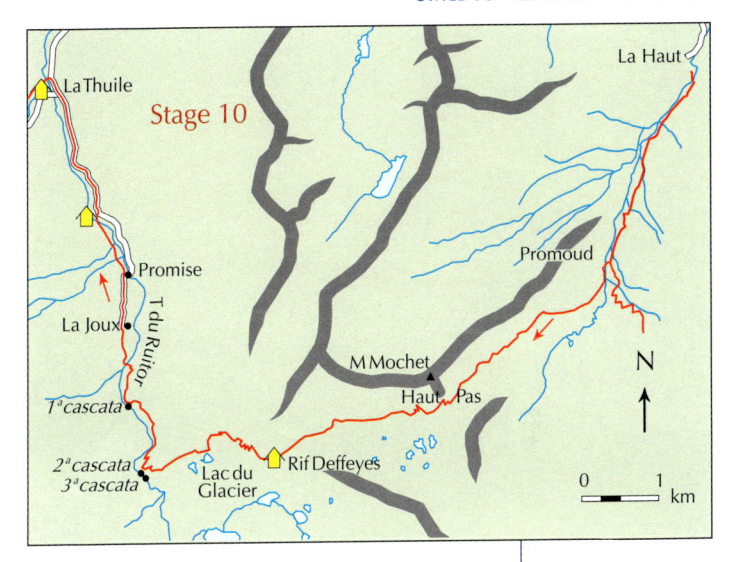

much steeper but the path is clear and trouble-free. Steps fashioned out of rock slabs also help you up to

> **2h15 – Haut Pas (2860m)** (Passo Alto), below Testa di Paramont. Rewarding views range back over Valle d'Aosta to the icy, snow-covered sprawl of Monte Rosa. The E side of the pass is dotted with pretty turquoise tarns, the Lacs des Usselettes.

The AV2 winds easily downhill W. Rock-ridden flanks are succeeded by huge glacier-smoothed rocks and a cool stream in Comba des Usselettes. Picnic spots abound, although it is helpful to remember that cotton grass means marshy terrain! Visible ahead is

> **1h – Rifugio Deffeyes (2500m)** tel 0165 884239 www.rifugiodeffeyes.it, CAI, sleeps 92, open mid-June to mid-Sept. Marvellously located facing the

*Lacs des Usselettes*

lakes and glaciers on the 3846m Rutior, which was first scaled in 1862 by English climbers Matthews and Bonney with Chamonix guide Michel Croz. It is well worth a stopover to explore the glacier at closer range on path n.16 that climbs SE towards Col de Planaval. The Grande Assaly is a distinct knife blade (SSW).

## A CAUTIONARY TALE

An age-old legend says this was once rich pasture. One day, the story goes, Christ was on earth to see what use man had made of the gifts bestowed on him. Disguised as a beggar he asked for a drink of milk, to which an ill-mannered shepherd retorted that he would rather pour his milk away than waste a drop on an old tramp – and rudely overturned a large pail, which drained away.

His iniquity incurred the wrath of the Almighty... White streams gushed from the earth itself, freezing along the way. A terrible wave of destruction submerged pasture and settlement alike leaving a young mother and her child as the sole survivors. The shepherd lives on beneath

## STAGE 10 – LA HAUT TO LA THUILE

the frozen mass, and it is his rage that makes the ice creak and shift. His tears of frustration flow out from beneath the glacier to form the lakes and waterfalls below. The bitter taste of the water comes from his soul, and the icy cold from his heart. No wonder it is undrinkable!

Nowadays the front of the Ghiacciao del Ruitor measures 3km across. Once much more extensive, the barrier collapsed on many occasions under the pressure of water and ice, causing terrible floods as far away as Villeneuve in Valle d'Aosta. Processions bearing the revered head of San Grato (see Walk 18) were a frequent local response. Luckily the mini ice age came to an end late 19th century. As the ice sheet retreated, it left hollows where lakes formed and these now colour the *combas* (long and narrow glacial valleys) with their turquoise hues.

The long descent now commences, on a pleasant mule track NW beside a lone Arolla pine into a vast valley trough of accumulated silt and the stunning **Lac du Glacier (2140m)**, backed by Col Lex Blanche at the head of Vallon de la Belle Combe. The path heads W up and down across rocks and into welcome shady wood with pink flowering alpenrose. It draws closer to the torrent that descends from the Ruitor glacier and there are soon marked detours off left to viewing points for the powerful waterfalls, marked **3ª *cascata*** then **2ª *cascata*** (third and second waterfall).

As volumes of glacial water thunder down the rock channel, sprays of cool suspended mist are whipped over unsuspecting visitors by the lighest breeze. Daring shrubs cling to overhanging holds, benefitting from the natural irrigation system.

The main path continues NW valleywards passing a deep-cut rock channel to an excellent viewing point for the **1ª *cascata*** (first waterfall). Not long afterwards you cross Torrent du Ruitor to

**2h15 – La Joux (1603m)**. Refreshments (cold drinks and ice cream), car park and mid-August shuttle bus to La Thuile.

Turn right along the tarmac. Immediately after a rise comes a sequence of signed shortcuts that keep you well away from the traffic. After touching on the road at **Promise (1515m)** you keep left of the torrent and take a forestry track past former Soggiorno Firenze.

The road is joined for the last leg through Villaret and down to the main road at

**45min – La Thuile (1447m)**. Grocery shops, bakery, ATM, year-round buses to Pré-St-Didier and trains. Chalet Alpina tel 0165 884187 or tel (mobile) 320 9225979 www.chaletalpina.it owned by friendly English speakers. B&B LT Horses & Dreams tel 390 11733 lathuiledreams@gmail.com. An excellent winter resort, La Thuile needs little introduction to British skiers. Its name derives from either a French version of 'tegula' – the stone roofing slabs – or Tullius Cicero, who was Caesar's lieutenant between 54 and 52BC during the wars against the Gauls.

## STAGE 11
*La Thuile to Rifugio Elisabetta Soldini*

| | |
|---|---|
| Time | 4h40 (opposite direction 3h45) |
| Distance | 18.4km/11.4 miles |
| Ascent/descent | 1156m/406m |
| Grade | 2 |
| Maps | L'Escursionista sheet 2, 1:25,000 or FMB 'Monte Bianco', 1:50,000 |

This second-last stage is straightforward if a little monotonous due to the lengthy climb; however, the abundance of unusual wildflowers (even orchids) is reasonable compensation. What's more, the highlight is a spectacular pass. After days and days of gradual approach with teasing glimpses, today the full glory of the Mont Blanc line-up will be revealed. Clear weather conditions are essential! At this point, anything else is instantly forgotten as

## STAGE 11 – LA THUILE TO RIFUGIO ELISABETTA SOLDINI

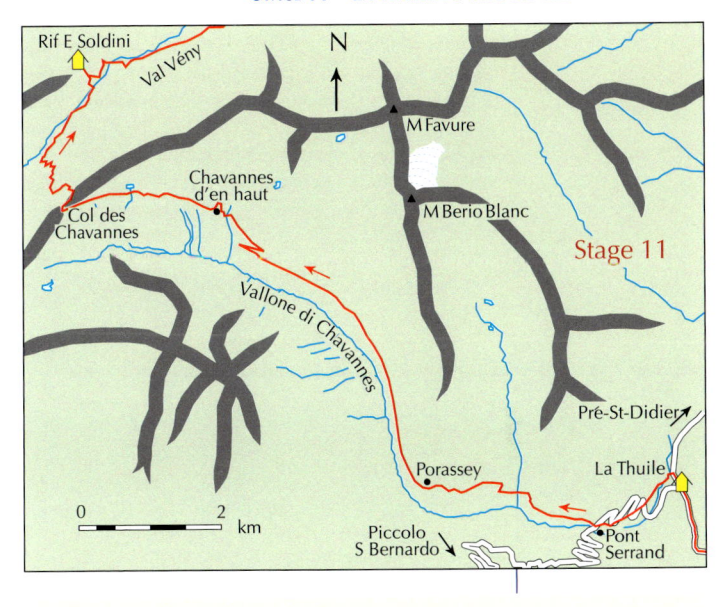

awe-inspiring Mont Blanc appears abruptly right in front of you. The ensuing gentle drop concludes at comfortable Rifugio Elisabetta Soldini, usually crowded with walkers on the Tour of Mont Blanc, so book well ahead in the high season. This is the AV2's last day of relative solitude.

On the main road at **La Thuile (1447m)** not far downhill from the post office and pharmacy, a clutch of yellow signposts marks the start of the ascent SW on an old paved track. It cuts the bends of the Piccolo San Bernardo road. About half an hour on, just before **Pont Serrand (1602m)**, walkers on the AV2 are directed off right (W) onto a narrow farm road (also the n.11), rather uninteresting despite the noisy crickets on the sun-beaten pasture. It leads past dairy farms and ends at **Porassey (1900m)**. A lane continues N through the narrow entrance of long, treeless but thickly flowered pasture valley, Vallone di Chavannes, which owes its appellation to a Late Latin name for kitchen premises

## GRAN PARADISO – ALTA VIA 2 TREK AND DAY WALKS

adjoining a summer farm. The bare slopes are the perfect hunting grounds for birds of prey. Climbing gradually, the route offers stunning views back to the Ruitor. Make sure you keep right at the 2244m fork for the slog up past the **Chavannes d'en haut (2424m)** farm huts. The final stretch means a traverse due W. The pass itself merits a slow approach as the ensuing outlook over **Val Vény** is simply breathtaking.

**3h40 – Col des Chavannes (2603m).** You probably won't even be vaguely interested in the chamois on the neighbouring cols, or the playful marmots, outdone by the dazzling mountains ahead with glaciers spilling every which way.

*Breathtaking views from Col des Chavannes*

Still on the n.11, the AV2 drops N, zigzagging easily down grassy slopes dotted with pretty alpine thrift. The broad base of Vallon de la Lex Blanche, site of an ancient Roman road, is quickly gained beneath the sheer limestone walls of the remarkable Pyramides

*Rifugio Elisabetta Soldini at the foot of the Lex Blanche glacier*

Calcaires. A delightful stroll right (NE) concludes with the brief climb past an old military hut and marmot burrows close to the immense ice fall of the Ghiacciaio de la Lex Blanche and

**1h – Rifugio Elisabetta Soldini (2197m)** tel 0165 844080 www.rifugioelisabetta.com, CAI, sleeps 80, open early June to late Sept. The showers come thanks to the turbine that harnesses the energy from the glacier. At this bustling refuge you'll encounter walkers from all over the world on the Tour of Mont Blanc (TMB).

## STAGE 12
*Rifugio Elisabetta Soldini to Courmayeur*

| | |
|---|---|
| **Time** | 4h30 (opposite direction 5h) |
| **Distance** | 12.7km/7.8 miles |
| **Ascent/descent** | 400m/1390m |
| **Grade** | 2 |
| **Maps** | L'Escursionista sheet 1, 1:25,000 or FMB 'Monte Bianco' 1:50,000 |

# Gran Paradiso – Alta Via 2 Trek and Day Walks

This concluding stage is fairly easy and a fitting conclusion to the AV2. The first part is a wonderful traverse with stunning views towards the Mont Blanc range and abundant extra time should be allowed for photographic stops. The latter section is a bit boring, although from Maison Vieille there's a jeep taxi or chair lift and then the brand new cabinovia can be ridden to Courmayeur, saving a couple of hundred dusty metres in descent.

**Note**: the unlucky few caught up in bad weather at Rifugio Elisabetta Soldini are advised to either wait it out or take the alternative valley route to Courmayeur (below).

Leave **Rifugio Elisabetta Soldini (2197m)** on the wide track to the valley floor NE where marshy watercourses make for lovely reflections and cloudy glacier-melt streams merge with clear water. Ahead, well below the soaring range is a curious, seemingly man-made ridge which attempts to bar the valley. Colonised by scattered trees, it is the line of lateral moraine shoved aside by the huge Miage glacier you are approaching. At the far end of **Lago Combal (2000m, 45min)** is cafè-resto and refuge Cabane du Combal tel 0165 1756421/339 6938817 www.cabaneducombal.com, sleeps 23, open June–Sept.

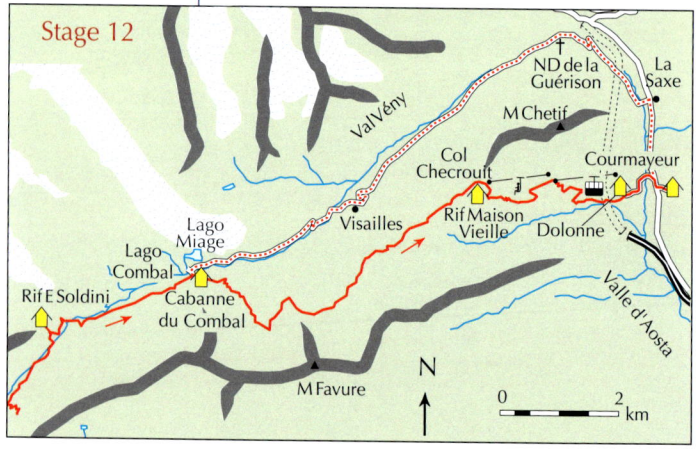

## STAGE 12 – RIFUGIO ELISABETTA SOLDINI TO COURMAYEUR

Soon the AV2 and TMB break abruptly right (E) shortly before a bridge. It is worth a 30min detour to see the constantly changing shape of murky, milky-grey Lago Miage, imprisoned by the encroaching moraine

*Getting ready to set out from Rifugio Elisabetta Soldini*

bulldozer and wall of ice that continues to topple trees in its path. Walkers intending to stay low and take the Val Vény route for Courmayeur part ways with the official AV2 route here.

### Valley route to Courmayeur (3h)
It is possible to bail out by continuing down the road to **Visailles (1659m, 1h15)**, whence a mid-summer bus to Courmayeur. However, Visailles is also the start point for a fascinating side trip to the Giardino di Miage, a weird pocket garden of larch trees trapped between the advancing arms of the ice mass. Then continue along the road past campsites and the odd hotel, with great views over to the Brenva glacier and of course Mont Blanc. A final landmark is the chapel of **Notre Dame de la Guérison**, an impassable barrier for the multitude of devils and witches banished to the high icy realms of Val Vény; curiously the chapel is also supposed to provide hope for young women in search of a husband. Around the corner on the main floor of Valle d'Aosta is upmarket La Saxe, close to **Courmayeur (1223m, 1h45)**.

If you stay with the AV2 from **Lago Combal**, it is a steady climb SSE past an abandoned summer farm and over pasture to the silent Alpe superiore de l'Arpe Vieille (2302m). A swing NW to detour round a spur of Monte Favure brings you to today's highest point (2400m, 1h20). It goes without saying that every step taken is rewarded with increasingly awesome views of the Miage glacier and Mont Blanc, along with amazing *aiguille* (rock needle formations) and everyone will inevitably stop for countless photographs. Contouring NE you walk through flowered pasture basins and soon begin to encounter ski lifts and pistes for use in winter. Across the valley is the sprawl of the mighty Brenva glacier at the rear of the Aiguille Noire de Peuterey. Gentle

## STAGE 12 – RIFUGIO ELISABETTA SOLDINI TO COURMAYEUR

*The Miage glacier and lake*

descent through light woodland leads to the broad saddle of

> **3h – Col Checrouit (1956m)** close to the rock triangle of **Mont Chetif**, lookout extraordinaire. An overnight stay or al fresco lunch can be enjoyed at **Rifugio Maison Vieille** tel 0165 809399 or (mobile) 337 230979 www.maisonvieille.com, sleeps 60, open mid-June to Sept, credit cards. Jeep taxi and luggage service to Courmayeur. Close-by is a midsummer chair lift that connects to the new Plan Checrouit gondola lift to Courmayeur.

The final descent is next, unfortunately lacking rather in interest due to the bulldozed aspect of the surrounding slopes in the name of skiing. Turn down right (E) on the broad dirt track, and the AV2 soon takes a path cutting across a ski piste to reach Plan Checrouit (1701m) and the *cabinovia* to Courmayeur. A dusty track suitable for 4-wheel drives continues in descent and there are soon views to Courmayeur below. Luckily a good signed path cuts through conifer woods, emerging at a playground in the fields alongside

> **1h15 – Dolonne (1210m)**, a charming village with a photogenic washing trough and hotels such as B&B Hotel Ottoz tel 0165 846681 www.hotelottoz.net

Clear signs point walkers through the maze of narrow streets and out to the main road. The Dora Baltea river is crossed and a short way uphill is the bus station and tourist office of cosmopolitan

> **15min – Courmayeur (1223m)**, with a wide choice of accommodation such as Pensione Venezia tel 0165 842461, Edelweiss tel 0165 841590 www.albergoedelweiss.it. Tourist office, shops galore, daily coaches to Aosta and beyond or through to Chamonix in France.

## STAGE 12 – RIFUGIO ELISABETTA SOLDINI TO COURMAYEUR

An exciting follow-up treat to the Valle d'Aosta's Alta Via 2 is a trip over the awe-inspiring Mont Blanc massif by a series of cable-cars. A local bus will drop you at La Palud on the outskirts of Courmayeur, from where you can make the 1h45 adventure all the way over to Chamonix in France (www.montebianco.com). Buses run back through the Mont Blanc tunnel, referred to as the Traforo di Monte Bianco in Italian.

*The Brenva glacier from Col Checrouit*

# DAY WALKS

*Ceresole Reale lake and the Tre Levanne (Walk 22)*

# WALK 1
## The Lillaz Waterfalls

| | |
|---|---|
| **Time** | 1h30 |
| **Distance** | 2.3km/1.4 miles |
| **Ascent/descent** | 150m/150m |
| **Grade** | 1 |
| **Start/finish** | Lillaz car park |
| **Map** | L'Escursionista sheet 10, 1:25,000 |
| **Access** | Summer buses from Cogne to Lillaz, a short drive. Otherwise 50min on foot via the marked 3.2km trail up the S side of the river. |

In the early summer months as rising temperatures melt the snow, torrents of foaming water come crashing down polished rock chutes into crystal-clear pools above the village of Lillaz. It is quite a sight even at other times of the year as the modest glaciers upstream ensure a constant supply.

Set in the popular Vallon di Cogne this is a straightforward circular walk with steep but short uphill stretches. It might seem excessive to devote a whole itinerary to these three waterfalls, but they are only revealed in their grandiosity – and 150m drop – once the path has been followed in its entirety. From Lillaz you only get a glimpse of the spectacle. No difficulty is involved but as several stretches are devoid of a protective guard rail and wind-borne spray makes the ground slippery, youngsters should be kept within reach. The quiet village where the walk starts has a modest choice of hotels, the odd food shop and many drinking fountains.

At the bus stop and car park at **Lillaz (1617m)** signposting for the 'cascate' sends you across the bridge through the small village. Take the first left through to Bar Cascate and a picnic area. The wide track follows the bank of the torrent virtually to the foot of the lowest fall. You climb up through shrub vegetation to several good viewing points. Then a path climbs the dry hillside temporarily away from the waterfalls, before curving back

*Gran Paradiso – Alta Via 2 Trek and Day Walks*

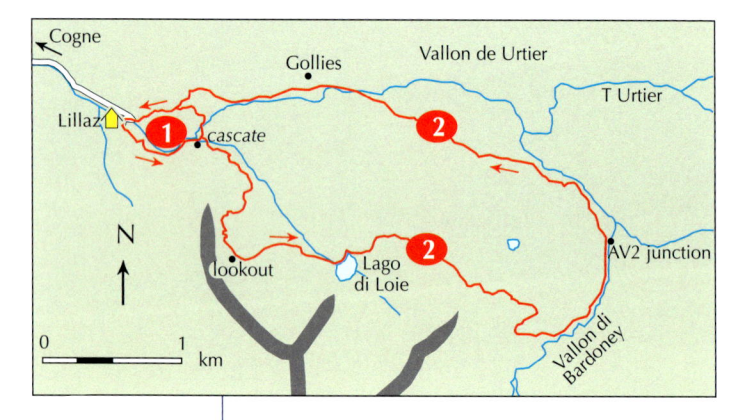

to the middle fall, with some crystal clear, azure pools. Not far above, along several stretches of wooden railing, is a giddy bridge over the torrent as it gushes through a picturesque rock channel.

From here continue uphill as the uppermost fall can be reached by way of a flowered meadow where martagon lilies abound. At the far end a short clamber leads down to an idyllic sheltered wooded area of tranquil pools among boulders. Weary feet can be instantly revived in the invigorating water. The highest fall is in the background, thundering out from a rock cleft.

To complete the circuit, instead of returning the same way, go back to the last bridge and turn right. Path n.14 leads between enormous glacially modelled rocks and light woodland to emerge in vegetable gardens on a hillside shrouded in rosebay willowherb. You soon join the main descent path from Vallon de Urtier. It comes out near the torrent once more, and not far down the dirt road is the car park you started from at **Lillaz (1h30)**.

---

**Lillaz:** B&B Jeantet Abele tel 0165 749129; Hotel Ondezana tel 0165 74248 www.hotelondezana.it. Some groceries.

*The top fall at Lillaz*

## WALK 2
*Lago di Loie*

| | |
|---|---|
| **Time** | 4h45 |
| **Distance** | 10.1km/6.2 miles |
| **Ascent/descent** | 760m/760m |
| **Grade** | 2 |
| **Start/finish** | Lillaz car park |
| **Map** | L'Escursionista sheet 10, 1:25,000 |
| **Access** | Summer buses from Cogne to Lillaz, a short drive. Otherwise 50min on foot via the marked 3.2km trail up the S side of the river. |

This beautiful, if lengthy, round trip in the Vallon di Cogne is suitable for all the family. The only difficulty is the steepish climb in the first part. As well as a variety of landscapes, there are plenty of panoramic points with marvellous views ranging as far as Mont Blanc. The lake area, brightly flowered, is a popular picnic spot and you may well see the herds of chamois that frequent the surrounding mountainsides and crests. During the return descent a detour can be made to take in the magnificent Lillaz waterfalls (see Walk 1).

For map see Walk 1

From the bus stop and car park at **Lillaz (1617m)** cross the bridge following signposts for the n.12 into the village. Following the signs for the 'cascate' you take the first left to Bar Cascate. Soon after a picnic area where the waterfall path continues alongside the torrent, n.12 starts its climb right (S). This is one of the few woods in the area and the Arolla pines, larch and fir provide welcome shade while alpenrose, bilberries and a variety of wild flowers brighten the undergrowth.

After 1h30 of steady and in parts steep climbing alongside a trickling waterfall, you emerge onto abandoned pasture near the overgrown and hardly recognisable ruins of Alpe Loie (2216m). Watching out for marmots, detour briefly to the right to an excellent **lookout**.

## WALK 2 – LAGO DI LOIE

In the distance towering beyond Cogne is the Grivola (W), while closer at hand is Punta Fenilia (SW), not to mention the collection of icy peaks S up the wild Vallon di Valeille. Above the tree line now, the clear path heads E across rubble for the final uphill stretch across easy open grass and rock terrain. ▶

Blue-green **Lago di Loie (2354m, 2h15)** nestles in a cup-shaped basin overlooked by grey points such as Punta di Loie (SSW). Its steeply sloping banks are covered by purple asters and black vanilla orchids, whereas the northern bank consists of glacially smoothed rocks. The area lends itself to picnics and even perhaps a (quick) swim. The name, also spelt Loye, comes from 'lex' locally used to refer to large slabs of rock used for roofing. Over the Vallon de Urtier are the abandoned mine buildings at Colonna, lofty and distant as a Tibetan monastery.

Path n.12 follows the side of the lake then climbs to another superb viewpoint from where Punta Tersiva is ENE and Mont Blanc WNW. As the path bears E, mostly on level ground, the peaks above delightful Vallon di Bardoney come into view, namely Punta Nera (E) then

Check the rocks above occasionally for solo male chamois at rest at a distance from the herds of females with their young.

*Lago di Loie*

Torre Lavina with its remnant glacier (SE). You descend towards a sea of green and gold vegetation in a shallow marsh. The path circles the wetter parts – beware of tempting but squelchy shortcuts through the cotton grass! Over a rise the path joins the main path along **Vallon de Bardoney (45min)**, a short distance from a summer farm (Alpe Bardoney). ◄ When the livestock are not around, marmots are more evident. The name Bardoney means a concentration of *Rumex acetosella*, otherwise known as sheep sorrel.

> The valley has widened considerably here providing lush green pasture.

Continue left (NE). The torrent rushes through deep passages before a lovely long drop into a blue pool. Further on is an **AV2 junction**, and from here on you share the path with the long-distance route, waymarked with a black and yellow triangle. It is NW now down through a mixed conifer wood alive with song birds. After intersecting a farm access dirt track just above Torrente Urtier, a wide bridge crosses the watercourse and reaches a hamlet. Keep left on the path (the wider track goes up to meet the restricted traffic road from Lillaz) and around to a signed path junction below the hamlet of **Gollies (1854m)**.

After ups and downs through tall vegetation, you emerge into the lower valley with a series of hidden waterfalls on your left. To see the justly well-known Lillaz *cascate* at close quarters, you can join the waterfall circuit (see Walk 1) as an alternative return by taking one of the branches off left. For the straightforward descent to Lillaz, keep on the path that winds down through scrubby wood to the valley floor near the torrent. A short stretch right along the road past a small hydro-electric power station brings you out at **Lillaz (1617m, 1h45)** where the walk began.

---

**Lillaz:** B&B Jeantet Abele tel 0165 749129; Hotel Ondezana tel 0165 74248 www.hotelondezana.it. Some groceries.

# WALK 3
## *The Money Glacier Terrace*

| | |
|---|---|
| Time | 5h |
| Distance | 12km/7.4 miles |
| Ascent/descent | 660m/660m |
| Grade | 2 |
| Start/finish | Valnontey |
| Map | L'Escursionista sheet 10, 1:25,000 |
| Access | Summer bus from Cogne to Valnontey (plenty of parking). On foot see AV2 Stage 4. |

A perfect first walk for a holiday in the Gran Paradiso, this is a superb and popular day outing in Valnontey. (Note: Valnontey is both the name of the settlement where the walk starts as well as the name of the valley.) Every ounce of effort spent in climbing the 650 steep metres to Alpe Money is fully repaid by the ample magnificence of the cascading Tribolazione glacier beneath the impressive chain of peaks from the Herbetet around to Gran Paradiso and Roccia Viva. Closer at hand it is not unusual to see ibex grazing on the high slopes even in midsummer.

While the initial part of the walk along the floor of Valnontey follows a wide easy track, the ascent to Alpe Money is steep and tiring in places and unsuitable for youngsters. Adverse weather would make it more difficult and hide the views. A final warning note: summer walkers should be aware that by the time they point their boots valleywards in the afternoon the upper streams may be swollen with snowmelt and crossing may become an adventurous endeavour. If the worst comes to the worst, you'll get wet feet.

From the bus stop and car park at **Valnontey (1666m)** are promising views S of glaciers, a mere hint of what is to come. A few minutes upstream at the bridge is signposting for Alpe Money, path n.22. Keep to the road along the left side of the wide, whitewater torrent to a campsite at the end of the driveable road. It is a pleasant stroll past clusters of huts including **Valmianaz (1729m)**, and through conifer wood.

## Gran Paradiso – Alta Via 2 Trek and Day Walks

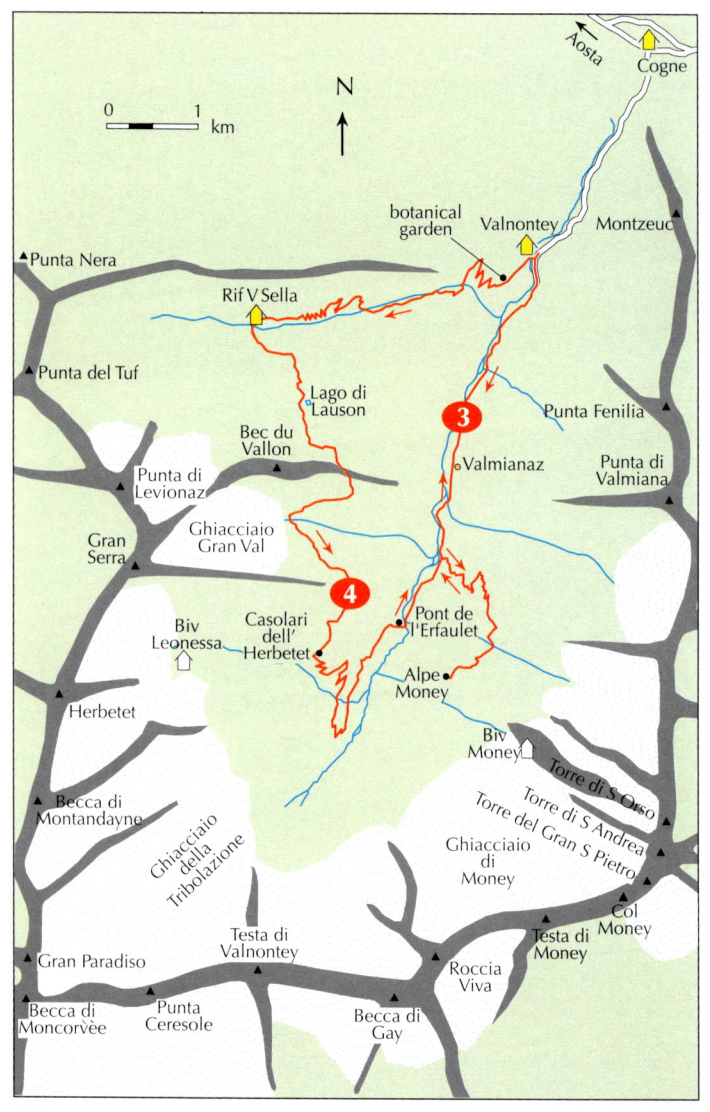

104

## WALK 3 – THE MONEY GLACIER TERRACE

*Upper Valnontey opens up during the ascent to Alpe Money*

## GRAN PARADISO – ALTA VIA 2 TREK AND DAY WALKS

After an hour you reach the turn-off left (still n.22) for the start of the climb. Stiff at times, it is initially a sequence of tight zigzags. Beneath the meagre larch trees are pink alpenrose, wine-red martagon lilies and fresh yellow gentians. At the tree limit there is a swing around left to the first of several moderately exposed passages with cables, then, after further climbing, the path resumes its southerly bearing to contour across dry mountainsides. The panorama verges on breathtaking but broadens even more as you proceed.

There's a rushing stream to be crossed on wobbly stones followed by ups and downs, then the junction for 'Biv. Money' (an extra 1h30 to the visible yellow bivouac hut set at 2872m – limited to energetic walkers with some climbing experience). Ignore the turn-off and keep on to the actual pasture area of **Alpe Money (2325m, 3h)**. The few abandoned shepherds' huts still standing are on a base of vast grey-brown slabs, lime green with lichen, of glacially smoothed rock – a reminder that the glaciers ahead once submerged the entire valley and ice masses slid along these flanks so high up from the present valley floor.

*At Alpe Money*

## WALK 3 – THE MONEY GLACIER TERRACE

According to legend, a ghostly horseman attired in green was once known to appear at Col Money and descend in great leaps and bounds over the glacier to play havoc with the milking cows, as revenge for a young shepherd being treated badly. On a calmer note, the place name is believed to be pre-Roman and is commonly found in Valle d'Aosta as a term for 'shared pastures'. Equivalents reputedly exist in the Irish *moin* and Gaelic *moneth*.

Due W over Valnontey are the Casolari dell'Herbetet, below the triangular peak of the same name, then in the near 180° sea of ice the rock protagonists are Gran Paradiso (SW), Testa di Valnontey (SSW), Roccia Viva (S), to name a few of these monumental mountains.

Return the same way to **Valnontey (1666m, 2h)**.

### Extension

It should be possible to make this walk into a circuit by proceeding beyond Alpe Money for a descent to the end of Valnontey at the foot of a glacier. However, this will depend on the state of the path across the moraine after Alpe Money, as well as a bridge in upper Valnontey being in place – it gets washed away nearly every spring. Do check beforehand as the flow can be very strong and crossing extremely dangerous without a bridge. The extension takes 1h15 from Alpe Money to the valley bottom, then 1h40 back to the start at the village of Valnontey.

---

**Valnontey:** Affittacamere La Clicca tel 0165 74157; Hotel Herbetet tel 348 0345002 www.hotelherbetet.com. Some campsites, a grocery shop and cafés.

## WALK 4
### The Casolari dell'Herbetet Traverse

| | |
|---|---|
| **Time** | 7h20 |
| **Distance** | 19km/11.8 miles |
| **Ascent/descent** | 1100m/1100m |
| **Grade** | 2–3 |
| **Start/finish** | Valnontey |
| **Map** | L'Escursionista sheet 10, 1:25,000 |
| **Access** | Summer bus from Cogne to Valnontey (plenty of parking), otherwise 50min on foot – see AV2 Stage 4. |

In the ever-popular valley of Valnontey, this route from Rifugio Vittorio Sella to the Casolari dell'Herbetet huts is one of the most spectacular itineraries in the whole of the Gran Paradiso. A rather narrow but well-maintained path stretches at a dizzy altitude of 2500m along the valley's western flank, while breathtaking panoramas onto the immense glaciers and icefalls improve with every step. As if further attractions were necessary, the zone is densely populated with wildlife – approachable ibex, chamois and marmots.

While the traverse itself is not suitable for beginners due to several exposed lengths (and inadvisable for anyone in low cloud or bad weather), the first stage as a return walk makes a wonderful family day trip. Summer reveals the area at its best without snow, although in the autumn the animals do move lower down in search of feed. An overnight stay at Rifugio Vittorio Sella is strongly recommended as this will give you more time for wildlife observation, late afternoon or early morning, near the refuge and the nearby lake.

What's more, of great interest en route is the Giardino Botanico Alpino 'Paradisia', the alpine botanical garden established in 1955 and named after Saint Bruno lily *paradisia liliastrum*. Encountered at the walk start a 5min stroll out of Valnontey, it boasts over 1000 labelled alpine plant species in an attractive 10,000m$^2$ of ponds and rockeries.

For map see Walk 3

Just up from the main car park and bus stop at **Valnontey (1666m)**, turn right across the bridge along Alta Via 2.

## WALK 4 – THE CASOLARI DELL'HERBETET TRAVERSE

The asphalt soon ends and clear path n.18 leads past the **botanical garden** to a waterfall with a wonderfully long drop. ▶ Wide zigzags lead steadily up the dry hot mountainside, meagre shade offered by the larches. After a timber bridge at 2000m the path climbs a grassy shoulder past old huts. Higher up it traverses to the right side of the watercourse amidst clumps of edelweiss. Ibex, not to mention noisy colonies of marmots devouring thistles and daisies, are common in this area, while chamois keep their timid distance.

The steady climb continues, eventually entering a vast basin. On the edge is the old picturesque royal hunting lodge, the scene of full-scale partying in the days of the Hunter King and now used by park rangers. Not far on is **Rifugio Vittorio Sella (2584m, 2h30)**. It was named after the highly acclaimed pioneer mountain and glacier photographer, whose black and white masterpieces from the late 1800s remain unsurpassed. Despite its great size, the refuge has a homely feel and walkers are fed well. Leftovers are appreciated by scavenging foxes under the cover of dark. After dinner on long light summer evenings a brief trek to Lago di Lauson is warmly recommended to

*Rifugio Vittorio Sella*

The wide, well-graded mule track is still used by the pack horse that plods this route loaded with supplies for the refuge.

109

## Gran Paradiso – Alta Via 2 Trek and Day Walks

observe the ibex and chamois watering and feeding, not to mention the extraordinary sight of young male ibex silhouetted on prominent rock outcrops, clashing horns in mock battle. In late summer, when higher pastures have been exhausted, great herds graze tranquilly on the grass flats in the vicinity of the refuge itself.

From **Rifugio Vittorio Sella** head SE across the torrent and along the paved royal game track (n.18B), winding in gradual ascent across damp grassy terrain and glacially smoothed rock slabs. The waters of picturesque tarn **Lago di Lauson (2656m, 30min)** reflect grandiose peaks and glaciers including the prominent Torre del Gran San Pietro (SE) and around to Roccia Viva (SSE).

After an easy walk around to the next point, the track comes to an abrupt end and a good but narrow path begins in brief descent. There is a reassuring, if short, length of chain at the very start, but the following 30min mean ups and downs with longish, moderately exposed stretches, requiring care and attention. Once around the midriff of Bec du Vallon, the path widens to enter SW the valley dominated by Gran Serra and Punta di Levionaz. After a stream crossing below the reduced Gran Vallon

*Taking it easy at Lago di Lauson*

glacier, the path continues S over rubble, guided by cairns. It climbs to an ample platform at 2600m, a magnificent viewing point. The icy masses of the majestic Ghiacciaio della Tribolazione seem only a stone's throw away SSW. The crest above it is punctuated by the Gran Paradiso peak (SW), the knob of Punta Ceresole (SSW), Testa di Valnontey and Gran Crou (S) and Becca di Gay barely (to their E).

The path now drops down the escarpment, a very brief narrow passage, to the similarly panoramic **Casolari dell'Herbetet** huts **(2435m, 2h)**, which are park property. The Herbetet peak is WSW from here. Its name, also used for the side valley, means 'small pasture area'.

The track which descends here has come through the ravages of many a winter in excellent condition, and its well-graded curves and built-up corners make it a delightful and relaxing walk. It snakes its way towards the valley floor, regularly visible a giddy 400m below, accompanied by swirling masses of delicately coloured butterflies attracted by the flowers. The air is heavy with the thundering of innumerable waterfalls as they descend from the semicircle of ice masses at the head of the valley.

The path turns decidedly S to avoid a steep cliff and into the welcome shade of larches, down to a bridge beneath a small waterfall, then to the nearby path junction with the main valley route where you turn left (2040m). Through the unusual profusion of green alder shrubs mixed with conifers, the path winds down to the bridge **Pont de l'Erfaulet (1830m)**. Here it crosses to the right side of the torrent and continues past several other path junctions and huts, widens to track-width and reaches the campsites and **Valnontey (2h20)** once more.

Rifugio Vittorio Sella tel 0165 74310 www.rifugiosella.com, CAI, sleeps 150, open Easter to end Sept
**Valnontey:** Affittacamere La Clicca tel 0165 74157; Hotel Herbetet tel 348 0345002 www.hotelherbetet.com. Some campsites, a grocery shop and cafés.

*Gran Paradiso – Alta Via 2 Trek and Day Walks*

*The path below Casolari dell'Herbetet (Walk 4)*

# WALK 5
## Punta Pousset – the local 'Gornergrat'

| | |
|---|---|
| Time | 7h30 |
| Distance | 13km/8.1 miles |
| Ascent/descent | 1600m/1600m |
| Grade | 3 |
| Start/finish | Cretaz |
| Map | L'Escursionista sheet 9 or 10, 1:25,000 |
| Access | Cretaz lies 1.5km N of Cogne, on the year-round bus route from Aosta. Car parking in village centre. |

The name for extraordinarily panoramic Punta Pousset comes from the French 'poucet' meaning thumb, as that is what it resembles when seen from the Cogne valley. Perhaps the first mountaineers to record their visit, Yeld and Coolidge writing in 1893, called it 'the Gornergrat of Cogne'. The wide-ranging views are unbeatable but there the resemblance to the Swiss peak ends, luckily, as neither the cogwheel train nor the floods of tourists is to be found here! The locals are well acquainted with Punta Pousset and the hefty 1500m climb involved, although the only crowds likely en route will be the wildlife – sizeable herds of chamois as well as ibex in the upper reaches of Vallone del Pousset.

Nothing more than a reasonable dose of stamina, healthy quadricep muscles and a good picnic lunch with plenty of liquid refreshment is required, as the itinerary is within reach of average walkers. Weather-wise a perfect, cloudless day is recommended.

One variant goes as far as Colle Posset and the unmanned hut Bivacco Gratton where an unforgettable overnight stay is ensured. Sleeping bag, cooking gear and food must be carried up, while trickling snowmelt water can be collected on the last leg to the col. However, be aware that the bivouac is popular with climbers en route to the northeast ridge of the Grivola, so may be crowded.

Make an early start from **Cretaz (1499m)**. Head across the two branches of Torrente Grand'Evyia and take

## Gran Paradiso – Alta Via 2 Trek and Day Walks

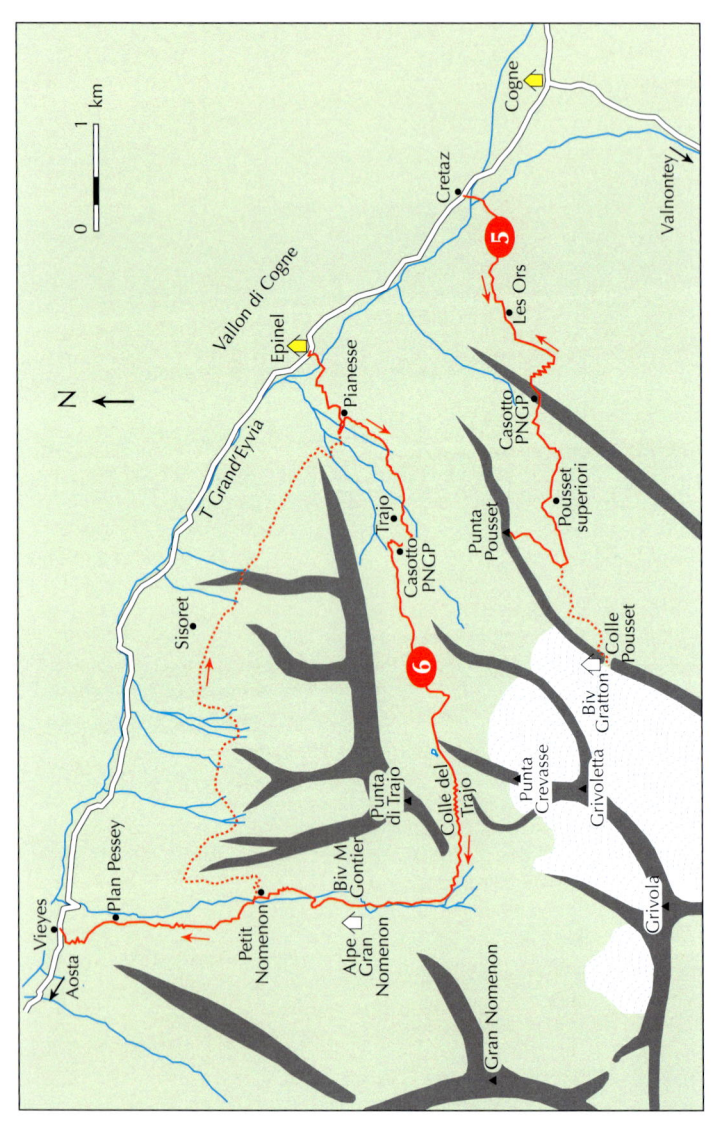

## WALK 5 – PUNTA POUSSET – THE LOCAL 'GORNERGRAT'

the marked path (n.26) that climbs steeply W through wood and pasture to the group of huts known as **Les Ors (1944m, 1h)**. Soon at a signed path junction, take the right branch onto the ridge which separates Vallone di Vermiana from Vallone del Pousset. You climb past a **Casotto PNGP** then down to cross the stream near the Pousset inferiori huts (2179m). The path continues W following the water, and crosses it again before climbing up to a vast area of glacially polished rock. Not far on you reach the old **Pousset superiori** huts **(2529m)**.

Keep on (right) above the buildings and proceed over a series of grassy terraces, where herds of chamois graze. At the next marked junction (2810m, 2h45), take the right branch for Punta Pousset.

### Extension to Colle Pousset (2h return)

From the 2810m junction, a fainter and more arduous path leads on W making its way across loose rock. A final series of zigzags brings you out at **Colle Pousset (3198m, 1h15)** and the compact metal box that is **Bivacco Gratton**, looking out over the icy spread of Ghiacciaio del Trajo. Inspirational.

It curves its way N, cutting across the steep grassy flank at the head of the valley. You eventually emerge on the crest, briefly W of the peak, where a clamber is all that separates you from the rocky point of **Punta Pousset (3046m, 45min)** and breathtaking panoramas. As Yeld and Coolidge put it, 'Cogne is at your feet', not to mention what appears to be the whole of the Alps as well. Return the same way to **Cretaz** (1499m) and allow around 3h.

---

Bivacco Gratton, sleeps 9, always open
**Cogne:** Ostello La Mine tel 0165 74445 www.ostellocogne.it; Hotel Stambecco tel 0165 74068 www.hotelstambecco.net; Residence Maison Pierrot tel 0165 749614 www.maisonpierrot.com

*Gran Paradiso – Alta Via 2 Trek and Day Walks*

# WALK 6
## Beneath the Grivola

| | |
|---|---|
| **Time** | 5h10 |
| **Distance** | 11.4km/7.1 miles |
| **Ascent/descent** | 1470m/1765m |
| **Grade** | 2–3 |
| **Start/finish** | Epinel/Vieyes |
| **Map** | L'Escursionista sheet 9 or 10, 1:25,000 |
| **Access** | Both Epinel and Vieyes are served by the daily year-round Aosta to Cogne bus, respectively 3.5km and 10km out of Cogne. Those with a car can park in either village and return by bus. |

The centrepiece of this superb route in the Vallon di Cogne is a 'beautiful maiden', the Grivola, a magnificent pointed peak first scaled in 1859 by a group of British climbers guided by a local game warden. The best viewing point is the Alpe Gran Nomenon in the second part of the itinerary. Second in magnificence if not fame is its elegant neighbour Mont Gran Nomenon which towers over the valley of the same name. For the geologically-minded the Grivola is composed of calcareous schist with ophiolites in contrast to the metadiorites that make up the Gran Nomenon.

The walk includes several long climbs and descents, rating average on the difficulty scale. Some snow can be expected around Colle del Trajo in early summer. The main route is a traverse. The alternative return to Epinel offers an excellent loop, although you should be warned that it is long (6h40) and tiring and only recommended for especially fit walkers. Otherwise with a little advance organisation – a phone call and trip to Aymavilles to collect the key – a memorable overnight stay can be made at comfortable Bivacco Gontier. Whatever the route chosen, all effort is amply rewarded by the superb views together with the excellent chance of observing herds of chamois and ibex at close quarters, along with birds of prey and ground nesters such as ptarmigan. The ibex tend to stay put on the path even at the approach of walkers, so you won't come far from bumping into one at times.

## WALK 6 – BENEATH THE GRIVOLA

An encounter with the giant 'ibex king', however, is the stuff of legends. Renowned as a sort of devil who uttered incomprehensible languages and kidnapped young children, his reputation was 'enhanced' after a challenge from the valley's fearless Hunter King. The encounter was brief as the hunter, blinded by bogus superiority, lost his footing and was sent hurtling down a ravine. In contrast humanitarian qualities are attributed to a gigantic golden eagle, erstwhile resident of the Grivola. According to a very ancient legend the local people, tired of suffering intense cold and mists, turned to the eagle for help. Eyes blazing flames, he set dead trees alight and thus introduced man to fire and heat.

From **Epinel (1470m)** take the wide bridge across Torrent Grand'Eyvia. There is signposting for path n.27, an unremitting climb SW beneath lovely conifers, whose needles make the going soft underfoot.

It is a good hour to the mechanised cableway and huts at **Pianesse (1743m)**. Keep left and up diagonally and the path soon emerges onto an open slope, to bear right across a rubble gully in the shade of Punta Pousset (S), with promising glimpses of the upper valley. A stretch of wood, mostly larch, and several stream crossings on is the brief detour to **Trajo (2040m)**. A minute away over the rise is the picturesque cluster of stone-slab roofed houses, built in timber that has weathered to a rich red-brown. Inhabited now exclusively by marmots and mice, they look NE to M. Emilius. ▶

Back on the main path, keep climbing to the **Casotto PNGP (2150m, 1h45)** set in a panoramic clearing. Out of the trees you climb around an old moraine ridge which descends from the diminutive Grivoletta glacier. Soon a steep rocky flank and unusual yellowish rock gully require some effort. This climb is somewhat deceptive as you do not reach the actual pass at the end but emerge onto a flattish pasture basin with a small lake, where herds of chamois are a frequent sight. The final leg is not as steep, although late-lying snow is possible. Eventually, **Colle del Trajo (2877m, 2h10)** opens up between Punta Crevasse (S) and Punta di Trajo (N),

For map see Walk 5

Also spelt Trajoz or Traso among other variations, the name refers to a route followed by shepherds with their livestock, probably a reference to the route to the upper col.

*Gran Paradiso – Alta Via 2 Trek and Day Walks*

*Casotto PNGP above Trajo*

## WALK 6 – BENEATH THE GRIVOLA

but it is of course the towering Grivola that demands attention.

The descent is straightforward and zigzags due W at first down a stony slope. This terminates in a beautiful grassy basin through which a trickling stream runs at the base of the imposing Grivola pyramid. An easy stretch right (N) drops to the **Alpe Gran Nomenon** and its cluster of recently refurbished huts, another Casotto PNGP and **Bivacco Mario Gontier (2315m, 1h)**. A welcoming stone and timber chalet (see below for information on collecting the key), it is anything but 'unalluring' as Yeld and Coolidge described it a century ago, although they did acknowledge the 'unrivalled position'. Here the Grivola can be enjoyed from yet another viewpoint, together with its brother Gran Nomenon (SW), not to mention the wide-ranging views to the north of the snowcapped ridges beyond Aosta.

Yellow arrows for n.5 wander N down the hillside. Cross to the right side of the stream and drop past a derelict hut to a bridge at **Petit Nomenon (1983m, 30min)**. The extention to Epinel starts here (see below).

Soon in a wood of silver fir where cushions of rare twinflower grow, the path winds pleasantly downwards. It eventually crosses back left beneath an impressive waterfall in a narrow section of valley, laden thickets of raspberries lining the path.

The next significant landmark is **Plan Pessey (1375m)**, a traditional medium-altitude farm. Go diagonally left here into the tall dense forest. The path curves easily down along old stone terracing on the final stretch and comes out on the road near a bus stop.

Just across the road is the quiet hamlet of **Vieyes (1114m, 1h30)**, whose few remaining inhabitants desert it during the sunless winter months. In addition to drinking water, a public phone and a bench, it offers visitors a small frescoed church.

### Extension: return on foot to Epinel (3h)

Turn right across the bridge and past the derelict huts for the faint path that soon climbs decidedly N through what appears to be the living room of a chamois colony. The way is narrow and exposed at times with countless ups and downs, ins and outs and the occasional plunging view into the valley and road below. About 50min from Petit Nomenon keep right at a fork for a short, aided section around a rock outcrop. Thereafter the going improves and you contour SE with frequent yellow arrows, bypassing the hamlet of Sisoret. Views reach over to the extensive Pila relief whereas Epinel soon comes into view still a long way off. In the Trajo valley once again, path n.27 is joined for the final leg downhill back to **Epinel (1470m, 3h)**.

---

Bivacco Mario Gontier (keys from Signore Gontier at Aymavilles (Saint Maurice 5) tel 0165 902259), sleeps 12, basic stove and cooking equipment, equipped with mattresses, blankets, wood stove, cooking gear. Water outside.
**Epinel:** B&B Le Traineau tel 0165 749624, 2002brenno@libero.it

# WALK 7
## Passo d'Invergneux and the Mines Circuit

| | |
|---|---|
| Time | 7h45 |
| Distance | 23.6km/14.6 miles |
| Ascent/descent | 1230m/1480m |
| Grade | 2 |
| Start/finish | Gimillan/Cogne |
| Map | L'Escursionista sheet 10, 1:25,000 |
| Access | Gimillan is a short midsummer bus trip from Cogne. Car owners can park in Gimillan or Cogne. |

While not included in the national park area, lovely Vallon de Grauson is well worth a visit. Wildlife is plentiful and there is a great variety of wild flowers, notably unusual concentrations of (protected) edelweiss. Paths and waymarking are generally clear, only in the solitary upper part prior to Passo d'Invergneux does orientation become a little problematic as path markers become a little scarce.

The descent route goes along Vallon de Urtier past Cogne's abandoned mines, preceded by a rather monotonous stretch of farm road. Should the mines not interest you, a more direct route to Lillaz is also possible, cutting nearly 2h off total walking time. Alternatively, the long walk can be split into two by overnighting at Rifugio Péradzà below the pass. The walk start, the quiet village of Gimillan (also spelt Gimmilian), is a winding scenic 3.5km above Cogne. It has several small hotels.

The final leg touches on the Colonna mines, said to be among the highest in Europe. They are located on the southern flanks of Monte Creyaz, whose pure magnetite mass used to yield an iron concentration of 55 per cent. Operations ceased in 1979 but historical records date back as far as the 15th century. Raw material was transported this far by sled in early times before the construction of the mechanised cableway. Since the 1920s it was forwarded to Aosta's iron foundry by narrow gauge electric train. The line tunnelled for 7km beneath the Punta del Drinc to terminate near Pila above Aosta, where another cableway took over. Adaptation of the railway line for passenger services is underway.

## GRAN PARADISO – ALTA VIA 2 TREK AND DAY WALKS

*A visit to the Colonna mines also makes an interesting day trip from Cogne. Follow path n.5 in ascent from the Cogne–Lillaz road below Moline. Allow 2h for the ascent.*

◀ From the car park and bus stop at **Gimillan (1787m)** head uphill to a batch of yellow signposts. Path n.8 threads its way NE between green meadows and alongside gushing irrigation channels. After brief changes of direction, the path passes a shrine and enters Vallon de Grauson. Torrente Grauson is crossed and farmhouses passed in a pastoral area. The next landmark is a flight of rock steps which climb alongside a waterfall, where a pause is in order to admire the view back SW to the glaciers at the head of Valnontey. Flowered terraces dotted with shepherds' huts and larch are followed by a metal cross and **Alpe de Grauson (2271m)**. The path soon crosses to the left side of the torrent where your passage may raise brilliant clouds of tiny metallic blue butterflies from their puddles. As the valley widens, glaciated Punta Tersiva is visible ESE and the signposted **Lussert junction (2415m, 2h)** for the renowned Laghi di Lussert (see Walk 8) reached. Graceful, pointed Grivola is in the distance (WSW).

Climb gradually E across lush green slopes into the peaceful, ample upper valley. In the vicinity of a cluster of basic huts (2418m) still used by shepherds, edelweiss are prolific together with purple asters and strongly

*Upper Valle de Grauson*

## Walk 7 – Passo d'Invergneux and the Mines Circuit

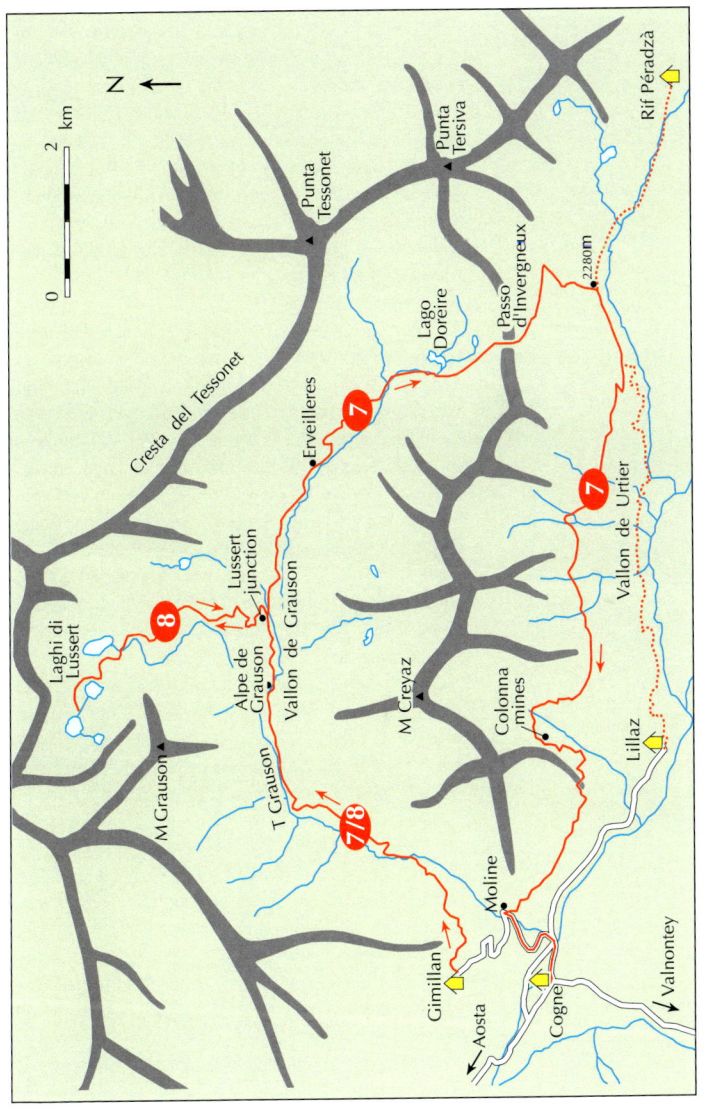

scented black vanilla orchids. You soon drop right nearer to the main torrent. The path as such disappears regularly and you are left with a very faint series of markings on the rare stones.

At the abandoned huts of **Erveilleres (2538m)** the pasture has been taken over by marmots and stinging nettles. Head right here but instead of the tempting torrent crossing, keep on the left bank and climb up to the ridge. Pointed stones have been set upright to guide walkers across the open expanses and shortly lead through an evocative oval of stones. With several side stream crossings, the route maintains a SE direction, up and down numerous hillocks to where another wider watercourse is reached. After this, the terrain becomes rockier and is covered with vast masses of glacially transported debris known as drumlins and kames. The path, clearer now, climbs due S to the westernmost end of **Lago Doreire (2731m)**.

Continuing SE you climb towards the pass through a distinctly different vegetation band – tiny, brightly coloured flowers for the most part. The alpine moon-daisies and ranunculus form fresh patches of white, tiny gentians contribute their intense royal blue and forget-me-nots an exquisite sky-blue. From a small lake on the left of the path, often dried up by midsummer, is an interesting view of the lower lake with an extensive dark NW-running ridge, Cresta del Tessonet, in the background. Helpful cairns lead you the final easy metres to wide flat **Passo d'Invergneux (2905m, 2h)** also known as Col des Hèvergnes, with its marvellous outlook. The name means 'wintering', a reference to the valley's first residents, shepherds from the Valle Soana who stayed over instead of returning home after the annual transhumance. Punta Tersiva is ENE, Punta Garin NW, Torre Lavin S, and you have a long clear view S down Vallon de Bardoney, not to mention Vallon de Urtier with its winding tracks and watercourses. Chances are that you'll have it all to yourself.

Narrow but initially clear, path n.10 drops across the flowered rubble slope which soon gives way to earth

## WALK 7 – PASSO D'INVERGNEUX AND THE MINES CIRCUIT

*Colonna mines*

and grass. It swings past the summer farm Invergneux (2520m) where a vehicle track leads down to a bridge and main dirt road at a **2280m junction** (1h) where it is possible to either go down to the village of Lillaz or branch off to a comfortable refuge for the night. If you want to break your walk overnight at this point, it is a further 30min left up the track to **Rifugio Péradzà (2526m)**.

A short way down the road you come to a junction. Take the turn-off right (on the n.10C). (If you wish to exit to Lillaz (1617m), stay on the road for the slightly monotonous 1h15, 6km walk down.) A tedious 1h on a broad gravel lane under power lines and enormous pylons follows. After Alpe Taverona (2388m) things cheer up as path n.5B takes over among thick clumps of edelweiss. Soon around a corner you see the huddle of constructions that made up the former mine. Raptors and cawing alpine choughs wheel around. The **Colonna mines (2387m, 1h30)** have long fallen into disuse and are fenced off. The upper reaches of the valley are pitifully bare in terms of vegetation, as trees fed the countless small-scale furnaces set up to smelt the iron ore before the mine was taken over by a large company and steel works established in Aosta.

The most straightforward route back to the valley is on path n.5 which heads SW at first descending over dry terrain with the odd, springy, dwarf mountain pine. The going is relentless and can be hard on the knees down to a path junction at Facette (1852m). From here on it is NW on a mostly level path which eventually joins a wide white vehicle track. This soon leads into **Moline (1576m)**, once a model mining village, which starts here and spreads downhill. The road goes down to the valley floor where you turn right for the centre of **Cogne (1534m, 1h15)**.

---

Rifugio Péradzà tel 0165 749111 or 384 6462534 www.rifugiosogno.it, sleeps 75, open mid-June to mid-Oct, credit cards, hot showers, traditional cuisine.
**Gimillan:** Hotel Grauson tel 0165 74001 www.hotelgrauson.it
**Cogne:** Ostello La Mine tel 0165 74445 www.ostellocogne.it; Hotel Stambecco tel 0165 74068 www.hotelstambecco.net; Residence Maison Pierrot tel 0165 749614 www.maisonpierrot.com

# WALK 8
## Laghi di Lussert

| | |
|---|---|
| Time | 6h20 |
| Distance | 19.8km/12.3 miles |
| Ascent/descent | 1120m/1120m |
| Grade | 2 |
| Start/finish | Gimillan |
| Map | L'Escursionista sheet 10, 1:25,000 |
| Access | Gimillan is a midsummer bus ride, or short drive, from Cogne. |

Delightful Vallon de Grauson and its high-altitude lakes are not included in the national park but make a memorable day trip. The pastures in the lower valley are still used for grazing, but, luckily for walkers, no road has been put in. Higher up, out of range of the grazing cows and their accompanying dogs, both marmots and shy chamois are likely, in addition to silent gliding raptors or even the lammergeier vulture, which local reports give as an occasional visitor. Charr, a type of alpine trout, survive in the chilly waters of the lakes. Paths and waymarking are clear and straightforward.

From the car park and bus stop at **Gimillan (1787m)** head uphill to a batch of yellow signposts. Path n.8 threads its way NE between green meadows and alongside gushing irrigation channels. After brief changes of direction, the path passes a shrine and enters Vallon de Grauson. Torrente Grauson is crossed and farmhouses passed in a pastoral area. The next landmark is a flight of rock steps which climb alongside a waterfall, where a pause is in order to admire the view back SW to the glaciers at the head of Valnontey. Flowered terraces dotted with shepherds' huts and larch are followed by a metal cross and **Alpe de Grauson (2271m)**. The path soon crosses to the left side of the torrent where your passage may raise

For map see Walk 7

*Lago superiore di Lussert*

## WALK 8 – LAGHI DI LUSSERT

brilliant clouds of tiny metallic blue butterflies from their puddles. As the valley widens, glaciated Punta Tersiva is visible ESE and the signposted **Lussert junction (2415m, 2h)** reached. Graceful, pointed Grivola is in the distance (WSW).

Turn up left (N) on path n.8A over a series of hillocks and rises and into the ample green expanse of this peaceful side valley. There are vast, flattened and glacially smoothed expanses of rock to be crossed and an incongruous oversized wall of rubble is invading the opposite side. ▶ Other signs of glacial action are the scooped-out armchair-shaped cirques that house the lakes. When you reach an unmarked junction keep straight on for the lowest and largest lake, **lago inferiore**, beyond the crest at 2721m (1h10).

Back at the junction, take the N fork for the second lake. The path, narrower and steeper now, climbs quickly up crumbly loose terrain then follows a ridge. It emerges at a squarish boulder on the broad shores of the inky middle lake, **lago intermedio** (2800m, 20min). Fed by a stream trickling from the upper lake, it occupies a steep-backed cirque amidst pink-red rock, blackened on the surface – yet another delightful flowered picnic spot.

For the final stretch to the top lake, follow the yellow arrows right along the shore to where clear marking guides you up the rocky walled sides and NW into the next desolate cirque. Snow persists well into summer at this altitude along with resolute gentians, daisies, oversized yellow-centred violets and tiny spiders around the shore of this highest lake (**lago superiore**, 2907m, 20min). Only the splash of the occasional fish surfacing breaks the silence. WSW is the pronounced peak of Punta Garin.

Return to **Gimillan (1787m)** the same way – allow 2h30.

> Although out of sight, a small glacier, Ghiacciaio di Lussert, is the force bulldozing that frontal moraine.

**Gimillan:** Hotel Grauson tel 0165 74001 www.hotelgrauson.it

# WALK 9
## Pondel's Roman Bridge

| | |
|---|---|
| **Time** | 1h30 |
| **Distance** | 5.3km/3.2 miles |
| **Descent** | 300m |
| **Grade** | 1 |
| **Start/finish** | Pondel turn-off/Viva |
| **Map** | FMB 'Gran Paradiso', 1:50,000 |
| **Access** | Alight from the Aosta–Cogne bus at the Pondel turn-off, about 4km above Aymavilles. By car you can drive all the way to the village of Pondel, but those intending to do the complete walk should park in Aymavilles. |

The great attraction of this fascinating itinerary is a marvellously intact, two-storey Roman bridge. It was built in 3BC to carry the unusual combination of water, people and goods across a deep gorge. A toll was charged for pedestrians and livestock using the covered lower passage and the top level was the aqueduct. The water was channelled down the westernmost bank of the Torrente Grand'Eyvia from Chevril, 3km up the valley. Traces of the excavated channels, originally 1–1.5m wide and 1.5–2m deep, are still visible along the rock face, although external suspended passages have disappeared.

The supply was destined for Roman settlements on the lower western flanks facing the main Aosta valley, probably for both agriculture and sand quarrying, but there are also stories about a gold mine. The bridge was a mere 'branch' from this main channel across to Pondel, once an important Roman stronghold against the local Salasso population who were holding out further up the Cogne valley.

According to the inscription on the keystone, Aimus and Avilius, two settlers from Padua, or perhaps Roman consuls, had the bridge built at their own expense and gave their names to the nearby village of Aymavilles.

Apart from the visit to the bridge, the walk is a novel and problem-free way of returning to Aymavilles. Note: a torch is handy through the short tunnel.

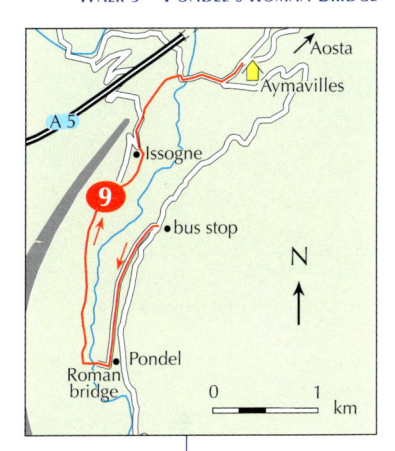

## WALK 9 – PONDEL'S ROMAN BRIDGE

From the signposted turn-off on the main road, it is a quiet walk down to the hamlet of **Pondel (890m, 15min)**, also referred to as Pont d'Ael (although experts say that this is incorrect as the name derives from 'ponticulus', meaning small bridge). Arrows guide visitors through the maze of houses to the astounding 50.5m long 2.20m wide bridge, spanning the torrent at a height of 61.5m. Once across the other side, the interior can also be explored by way of side entrances.

Turn right on path n.2A heading N, high above the torrent. It follows abandoned stone terracing which once supported vineyards and orchards. The hot dry terrain is now the domain of crickets and butterflies. As well as interesting snow-capped ridges visible NE beyond Aosta, there are good views to the bridge, backed by the distant Grivola and a glimpse of glaciers.

After 15min of gradual ascent, the path branches up left diagonally, heading for a seemingly impassable rock barrier. Here, surprisingly, you encounter a 60m-long tunnel excavated out of the rock by World War I Austrian POWs (also to be thanked for the Cogne road). It does have one window but a torch is useful.

The path zigzags down the steep flank then resumes its northerly direction and feels a little exposed for a brief stretch. Crumbly side gullies are crossed on wooden bridges and you may surprise some chamois in the mixed woods. After skirting a vineyard and crossing a torrent, the path emerges alongside the apple and pear orchard belonging to a very old rambling farmhouse, **Issogne (50min)**.

Take the surfaced road downhill through masses of blackberries. Waymarking for the old path points off right. Take this and drop quickly between old walls and a thick chestnut wood with scavenging squirrels and noisy

131

*The Roman bridge at Pondel*

black grouse. Foxes and wild boar are not unknown here. As you round the hillside on the edge of the main Aosta valley, the fanciful turrets of the 11th-century castle of Saint Pierre appear ahead. Down through the manicured vineyards, you emerge onto a narrow surfaced road. Once over the bridge there are apple and pear orchards as well as houses at Moulins, then you bear right and soon reach the main square of **Aymavilles (641m, 25min)**. As well as a bus stop, shops and bars, there is a modest villa-cum-castle and the Church of St Léger with an unusual 18th-century *trompe l'oeil* frescoed façade.

**Aymavilles:** B&B Le Clair de Lune tel 320 0645237 www.bedandbreakfastleclairdelune.it

## WALK 10
### *The 2205m Mont Blanc*

| | |
|---|---|
| Time | 4h40 |
| Distance | 11km/6.8 miles |
| Ascent/descent | 1050m/1050m |
| Grade | 1–2 |
| Start/finish | Rhêmes-Saint-Georges |
| Map | L'Escursionista sheet 3, 1:25,000 |
| Access | Rhêmes-Saint-Georges in Val di Rhêmes is connected by an infrequent, year-round bus service from Aosta. |

At the northernmost opening of Val di Rhêmes this modest Mont Blanc is easily 'scaled' without ice-axe or crampons. Its isolated and commanding position at the start of Val di Rhêmes gives it sweeping, virtually uninterrupted views over the Valle d'Aosta taking in the spectacular Mont Blanc to Grandes Jorasses line-up, the Grand Combin, the Grivola and Gran Paradiso, to mention but a few.

The smaller Mont Blanc owes its name to the light colour of its calcareous rock. The walk used to be a jealously guarded local secret but this appears to have changed since the Pope reportedly came here on one of his recent Valle d'Aosta summer sojourns. Walkers can generally count on the access tracks being clear of snow as early as May and as late as November due to its extended exposure to the sun. The first stretch is an easy path which becomes a wide dirt track, making it feasible for anyone who can manage the climb of 1050m. Added attractions are the stable colony of ibex around the peak and a good chance of sighting chamois in the woods.

A short distance uphill from the bus stop at **Rhêmes-Saint-Georges (1159m)**, take the turn-off for **Coveyrand**. The narrow asphalt road climbs NE to the hamlet's Ecole Maternelle in a small square and parking area at 1234m. Head uphill on the road, which soon becomes a dirt track closed to unauthorised traffic. Not far on you turn right at a prominent fork. (Champromenty and

*Gran Paradiso – Alta Via 2 Trek and Day Walks*

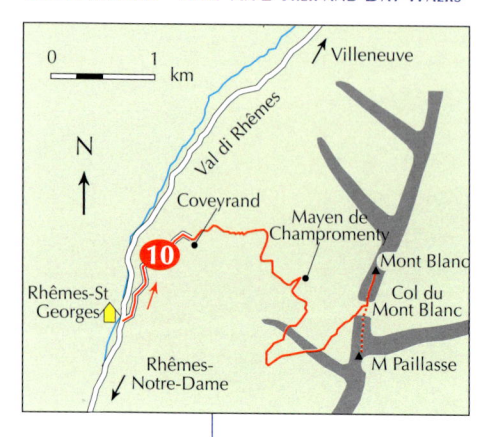

Mont Blanc are signposted to the left along the road but this is a much lengthier variant.) The path (formerly n.301) is followed through light vegetation and across a stream, cutting up through bird-filled conifer forest and climbing steadily. As path n.3, it intersects the road three times before reaching picturesque summer farm, **Mayen de Champromenty (1813m)**, complete with characteristic stone-slab roof, turret and drinking water. The dialect designation *mayen* means a medium-altitude farm that can be utilised as early as May to provide the livestock with fresh grass while waiting for the snow to melt on the higher altitude pastures (where the huts are known as *montagnes*).

No-one should expect shepherds to live in uninteresting places and the outlook here is simply wonderful: although limited to the Val di Rhêmes, the view takes in

*At Champromenty*

pointed Becca di Tey (SSW), the Grande Rousse (immediate S) and the rest of the ridge.

Now continue up the wide farm vehicle track, marked as n.4, swinging S then NE. There are thick banks of pink alpenrose beneath thinning larch, a meagre cover for the shy chamois who usually betray their presence by dislodging stones. The views open up gradually as you head for a modest mount due N with a distinctive light colour. At the wide saddle of **Col du Mont Blanc (2170m)** leave the track and head for the Casotto PNGP. Just before it, take the path left around the rocky outcrop where a sizeable herd of ibex is regularly to be found. After a grassy slope and then a scramble, you are on the highest point of breathtaking **Mont Blanc (2205m, 2h30)**. The view ranges virtually uninterrupted from W to ENE (Mont Blanc NW) then resumes SE with the slender sharp points of the Gran Nomenon and Grivola, followed by Gran Paradiso and Ciarfaron to the S.

### Extension to Mont Paillasse (1h15 return)

For those with extra energy to burn, an even more extensive outlook can be gained in exchange for a further 250m (40min) in ascent. From Col du Mont Blanc, rejoin the track and proceed S along the wide grassy ridge then up to 2414m and the top of Mont Paillasse and its trig point.

From **Mont Blanc** return the same way to **Rhêmes-Saint-Georges (2h)**. A feasible variant is to take the road down from Champromenty. It makes for a more leisurely descent if a fair bit longer and is surfaced a good part of the way.

**Rhêmes-Saint-Georges:** Camping Val di Rhêmes tel 0165 907648 www.campingvaldirhemes.com with bungalows for rent. Nearest hotel accommodation: Rhêmes-Notre-Dame. (See Walk 14.)

*Gran Paradiso – Alta Via 2 Trek and Day Walks*

# WALK 11
## At the Foot of the Gran Paradiso

| | |
|---|---|
| **Time** | 6h |
| **Distance** | 16km/9.9 miles |
| **Ascent/descent** | 1210m/1120m |
| **Grade** | 2 |
| **Start/finish** | Pravieux/Pont |
| **Map** | L'Escursionista sheet 9, 1:25,000 |
| **Access** | Valsavarenche is served by buses from Aosta all year round as far as Eaux Rousses, extending a further 5km to Pont in summer, where the road terminates. Pravieux is midway between Eaux Rousses and Pont. Drivers can park at either start or finish. |

This excellent route in Valsavarenche includes a superb high-altitude traverse with sweeping panoramas. It connects two important and popular refuges, both essential bases for mountaineers heading for the Gran Paradiso. At 4061m and the only peak wholly within Italian territory that exceeds 4000m, its first recorded ascent was by English climbers JJ Cowell and W Dundas with French guides Michel Payot and Jean Tairraz in 1860. In this day and age the ascent enjoys enormous popularity, consequently an overnight stay in either of the huts usually means being woken at an ungodly hour as groups set out for the summit. Of the two, the modern Rifugio Chabod is quieter and more comfortable. Advance booking is strongly recommended in both cases, especially in midsummer and weekends should be avoided where possible.

This is one of the best walks for families as it is problem free; however, the length and steep climbs should be taken into account. Doing it as a single day means a rather long haul. Wild animal sightings are guaranteed as huge numbers of ibex inhabit these flanks. The most popular section is the Pont–Rifugio Vittorio Emanuele II path, while the traverse itself is relatively untrodden.

From **Pravieux (1871m)**, follow the clear signpost for Rifugio Chabod, path n.5, over the wide bridge then E.

## WALK 11 – AT THE FOOT OF THE GRAN PARADISO

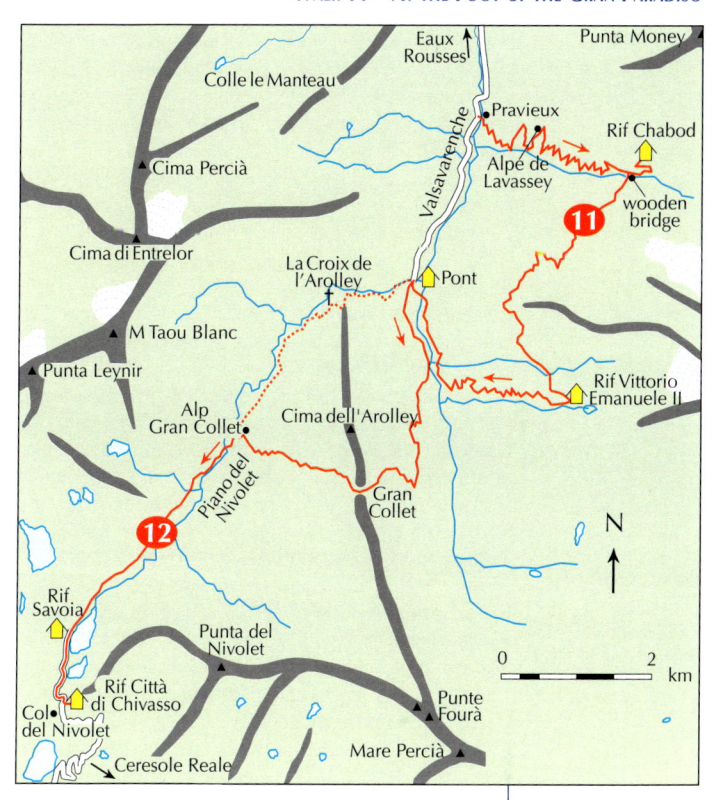

You pass close to the rear of characteristic vaulted farm buildings, and a masterpiece of alpine path construction awaits. A mule track with carefully built-up corners climbs in regular curves, keeping to the left of a cascade, out of sight. Livestock have been escorted to summer pastures along this route for centuries. The conifer wood is alive with squirrels, nutcrackers and even the occasional lone male chamois.

At 2194m is a clearing with the modest farm **Alpe de Lavassey**. There are ample views of the opposite flanks of Valsavarenche, right up to Punta Basei (SW). Keep right at the path junction (ignore n.5A to Bivacco Sberna) and, as the larch trees thin, immense expanses of glacially smoothed rock come into sight, often with ibex standing sentinel on the crests. Fawn-coated chamois graze on the grass flats, ready to flee at any hint of danger.

After a good few hours winding and plodding, well above the tree line, a **wooden bridge** is passsed (n.1A turns off right for the traverse) and shortly afterwards is the refuge's turbine at the base of a cascade. A wide path climbs diagonally left up the final 100m to a platform and **Rifugio Chabod (2750m, 2h30)**. It occupies a simply magnificent position facing the northwestern flank of the Gran Paradiso (SSE), Piccolo Paradiso and then the dominating Becca di Montandayne (SE). The modern but simple refuge was named after a local inhabitant who became the first President of the Valle d'Aosta's autonomous government following World War II. Hours can be spent just observing the large herds of ibex that haunt the rock slabs on the opposite bank of the torrent.

Return to the **wooden bridge** and cross it left (S) for path n.1A in gradual descent SW. Spreads of moraine are touched on, including a funnel formed by lateral ridges below the retreating blue ice belonging to the Laveciau glacier. The name is derived from a dialect word meaning a place where salt was left for ibex and chamois to lick. After a second bridge over a tumultuous freezing cold stream you face a series of ups and downs as you round the Testa di Montcorvé. After a shoulder, you then cross a desolate stone-filled valley. If you look upwards every now and again, you'll catch ibex youngsters peering down from high rock perches.

Back on grass once more, at a path junction, the next *rifugio* is visible so it is logical to take the left branch for the final climb. (The wider track which continues straight ahead (S) eventually joins the main descent path.) You climb over smoothed rock slabs and then meagre pasture punctuated with gentians and oxe-eye daisies.

**Rifugio Vittorio Emanuele II (2732m, 2h)** stands just back from the shore of a small tarn, Moncorvé. The position is superb. Virtually due S is slender pointed Becca

## WALK 11 – AT THE FOOT OF THE GRAN PARADISO

di Monciair, while SE is the rounded form of La Tresenta and the impressive north wall of the Ciarforon is SSE. **Note**: The water here is not suitable for drinking.

The original refuge, the small hut still used as an annexe, was inaugurated in 1884 in honour of the Hunter King and at the cost of 6160 lire. Writing in 1893, Yeld and Coolidge described it as 'very commodious (5 rooms) and very well fitted up in all respects, so that it is probably the best Club hut in the Western Alps, and has therefore been named "The Palace"'. The popularity of this area and the Gran Paradiso ascent made a more spacious building necessary. The decision was taken in 1927 but the work not completed until 1961! ▶ With binoculars, you will be able to spot numbers of reclining ibex on any of the surrounding ridges, while chamois graze on the lower reaches and keep their distance. The alpine choughs can almost be hand fed.

The clear well-trodden track (n.1) heads W downhill. After the initial debris-covered flanks, grass and earth reappear, but it is the ubiquitous glacially smoothed and lichen-stained slabs that dominate. The easy path means you have time to enjoy the vast landscape and

*Rifugio Vittorio Emanuele II comes into sight during the traverse*

The strange, curved, metallic building is rather incongruous but some consider it a perfect fit for its setting among the moraines.

*Rifugio Vittorio Emanuele II*

views over Valsavarenche. Late afternoon will guarantee an encounter with the laden pack mules that supplement the refuge's start-of-season helicopter drop of foodstuffs.

After endless curves the path enters a larch wood with bilberries and alpenrose as undergrowth. Once down on the actual valley floor in the vicinity of an old vaulted hut and close to the torrent, it is a final stroll right (N) along to the bridge crossing for **Pont (1960m, 1h30)** and the enormous car park, campsite, shop, as well as a couple of hotels and restaurants scattered down the road.

---

Rifugio Chabod tel 0165 95574, sleeps 85, open 15 June to 15 Sept www.rifugiochabod.com; Rifugio Vittorio Emanuele II tel 0165 95920 www.rifugiovittorioemanuele.com, CAI, sleeps 152, open mid-March to mid-Sept

**Pont:** Hotel Gran Paradiso tel 0165 95454 www.hotelgparadiso.com; Hotel Genzianella tel 0165 95393 www.genzianella.aosta.it

## WALK 12
### Over Gran Collet to Col del Nivolet

| | |
|---|---|
| Time | 4h50 |
| Distance | 10.5km/6.5 miles |
| Ascent/descent | 1090m/440m |
| Grade | 2 |
| Start/finish | Pont/Col del Nivolet |
| Map | L'Escursionista sheet 9, 1:25,000 |
| Access | Pont can be reached by midsummer bus from Aosta. Col del Nivolet is served by a shuttle bus to and from Lago Serrù (Suns and public holidays, July to Aug), with extensions to Ceresole Reale. From there a year-round line goes as far as Pont Canavese and the railway. The narrow 16km Ceresole Reale–Col del Nivolet road is kept open 15 May to 15 Oct but closed to private vehicles on Suns and public holidays from 9am to 6pm. |

With a departure from the head of Valsavarenche, this itinerary climbs quickly to the spectacular Gran Collet pass, an especially rewarding way to enter the Piano del Nivolet. It also serves as a link between the northern Valle d'Aosta and the southern Piemonte sides of the Gran Paradiso National Park. The vast *altopiano* lying 2300m to 2500m above sea level is famous for the unrivalled spectacle in early summer when it is transformed into a sea of white and yellow by the buttercup *ranunculus pyrenaeus* and early-opening pasque flowers. It is an ancient glacial valley where silt transported by water has accumulated over time, with a transformation into fertile grasslands, appreciated by the rotund cows and sheep grazing there.

Thankfully a link road proposed in the 1960s related to a hydroelectric project never materialised, leaving the vast peaceful plateau for the enjoyment of livestock, marmots, walkers and other wildlife. A curious 'negative' note to this pastoral idyll comes from the shepherds who report attacks on lambs by golden eagles who single them out as easier prey than marmots. At the southernmost extremity is the Col del Nivolet road pass which offers access to the southern Piemonte side of the park, and surprisingly dramatic contrasts in landscape.

*Gran Paradiso – Alta Via 2 Trek and Day Walks*

This Gran Collet route is less popular than others in Valsavarenche and extra care should be taken not to disturb the large herds of both chamois and ibex and their young in the upper reaches of the valley. The views are incomparable, thanks to the proximity of the Gran Paradiso range. While the walk is not particularly difficult, the climb is steep and relentless, requiring good stamina. Moreover walkers should be aware that the pass may be blocked by snowdrifts well into the summer and an easier direct route is given to Col del Nivolet via La Croix de l'Arolley. An excellent round trip for those wishing to return to base (4h20) is Pont–Gran Collet–La Croix de l'Arolley–Pont.

For map see Walk 11

*Superb views to Gran Paradiso on the ascent to Gran Collet*

From **Pont (1960m)** walk through the campsite and follow the path S along the right bank of the torrent up Vallone di Seyvaz. Not far along, a narrow path breaks off right, marked by a yellow 2A, easy to miss. The climb is immediately stiff and the path narrow but good. Bearing almost imperceptibly SSW it heads for abandoned Alpe de Seyvaz (2358m), now home to marmots. At the head of the valley the Grand Etret glacier is visible, overshadowed by the Denti del Broglio (SSE).

## WALK 12 – OVER GRAN COLLET TO COL DEL NIVOLET

*Carpet of white ranunculus on Piano del Nivolet*

'Gran Collet' painted on a rock indicates the path which continues S a little longer. Waymarking also consists of the occasional 2A in yellow and white stripes or arrows. Turning W soon, you climb through a series of grassy basins, many of which will be occupied by ibex females and their inquisitive young who often spy on visitors from giddy outcrops. At the last ample terrace preceding the pass, visible now, a photographic stop is called for if you haven't already exhausted the possibilities (note that from the pass itself the view is partially obscured). From ESE to NE is the stunning sweep taking in Ciarforon, Tresenta, the shiny metal roof of Rifugio Vittorio Emanuele II beneath Gran Paradiso, then Piccolo Paradiso and Becca di Montandayne.

The final stretch cuts up the right flank of a dirt-specked snowy slope to the ample saddle of **Gran Collet (2832m, 2h30)**, where a squawking flock of alpine choughs awaits your crumbs.

Although not on a par with the preceding valley, interesting new views W and S range over the ample Piano del Nivolet, dominated by Mont Taou Blanc (WNW), and Punta Basei (WSW), interspersed with small glacier and snow pockets.

The path heads WNW down a dirt slope and back onto grassy terrain bejewelled with piercing blue gentians, and riddled with marmot burrow entrances as well as a few lakes. Where the path as such disappears, cairns point the way across the grassy slopes to wind down easily to the Piano del Nivolet, where you turn left to join the path from Pont in the vicinity of the ruined huts of **Alpe Gran Collet (2403m, 40min)**.

A short distance along SW, the broad path climbs briefly and several bridges cross the meanders of the torrent among densely flowered high-altitude meadows. Further up you join the surfaced road.

The two sizeable Laghi del Nivolet are close-by, then the first of the two huts, **Rifugio Savoia (2532m)**. Originally one of the king's hunting lodges, it is more a modest hotel nowadays with souvenirs, tourists and a large car park and lacks the mountain refuge atmosphere. (An overnight stay includes sheets and a hot shower.) Not far up the road and off to the left in a panoramic position is quieter **Rifugio Città di Chivasso (2604m)**, originally built for military purposes around 1940. The helpful custodian is highly knowledgeable about the area and a well-stocked library is available for guests. ◀ The building is powered by solar panels and

The only 'but' concerns the water – in short supply as it is pumped from a nearby lake, and unsuitable for drinking.

*Waiting for dinner at Rifugio Città di Chivasso*

## WALK 12 – OVER GRAN COLLET TO COL DEL NIVOLET

a hot showers possible. With luck you might catch a glimpse of the ermine which turn up after dinner hoping for scraps.

The **Col del Nivolet (2612m, 1h20)** is only a matter of minutes up the road, and, together with the marvellous angle onto Punta Basei (W) from here, a whole new world of stunning mountain ranges – most notably the three Levanne peaks (SSE) bordering France and its Vanoise National Park and lakes – opens up at your feet. The name Nivolet comes from an old word for snow.

### Alternative via La Croix de l'Arolley (1h40)

At **Pont (1960m)** take the signposted path (n.3) from the rear of Hotel Gran Paradiso. It climbs easily W through larch wood and alpenrose close to a waterfall before the gradient increases dramatically as you zigzag up the steep escarpment on a reinforced path to the prominent old wooden cross, **La Croix de l'Arolley (2310m)**.

Brief ups and downs lead across expanses of rock polished by the slow passage of an ancient glacier and lovely picnic spots present themselves by a gushing torrent as you head SW. Keeping to the left side of the open valley, Piano del Nivolet, the next landmark is the stone skeleton of the buildings of **Alpe Gran Collet (2403m)** just off the path, and here you join up with the main itinerary.

---

**Col del Nivolet:** Rifugio Città di Chivasso tel 0124 953150
http://rifugiochivasso.altervista.org, CAI, sleeps 44, open late June to late Sept; Rifugio Savoia tel 0165 94141 www.rifugiosavoia.com, sleeps 60, open 15 June to 30 Sept
**Pont:** Hotel Gran Paradiso tel 0165 95454 www.hotelgparadiso.com; Hotel Genzianella tel 0165 95393 www.genzianella.aosta.it

## WALK 13
### The King's Path in Valle delle Meyes

| | |
|---|---|
| Time | 4h30 |
| Distance | 10.5km/6.5 miles |
| Ascent/descent | 730m/730m |
| Grade | 2 |
| Start/finish | Pont |
| Map | L'Escursionista sheet 9, 1:25,000 |
| Access | Valsavarenche is served by buses from Aosta all year round as far as Eaux Rousses, with midsummer runs extending a further 5km to Pont, where the road terminates. Pravieux is midway between Eaux Rousses and Pont (parking available). |

After the ascent to the solitary Valle delle Meyes high above Valsavarenche, with marmot, ibex and eagle viewings guaranteed, this route heads along one of the best preserved and the most panoramic stretches of royal game track in this northern section of the park. It affords a magnificent sweeping panorama over Valsavarenche to the Gran Paradiso peaks in their snow and ice setting. No particular difficulty is involved and this walk is perfectly suitable for energetic family groups. It also lends itself to several excellent variations. For example, it can form a link with Stage 6 of Alta Via 2 by heading off N via Colle le Manteau to Lac Djouan and Eaux Rousses. It can also be extended S to Col del Nivolet (see below).

At **Pont (1960m)**, a short distance downhill from the main car park next to the Hotel Genzianella, is the start of a wide track. It was to have been an access road over S to Col del Nivolet for the purposes of a late 1960s mammoth hydroelectric project which never materialised. This initial 3km stretch (marked n.4), totally abandoned nowadays, constitutes a convenient and panoramic access for the Valle delle Meyes. Although closed to 4-wheeled traffic, it is popular with mountain bikers.

## WALK 13 – THE KING'S PATH IN VALLE DELLE MEYES

After several wide curves, it heads decisively N to a short, well-lit tunnel. Just as the second tunnel is reached, where the road turns left, take the path off straight ahead (faint n.4 marking). Ignore the yellow arrows for a mountain bike itinerary and head up diagonally left on the upper branch to a shrine near old farm huts (Meyes di Sotto, 2275m). The view E across the valley to the Gran Paradiso and surrounding peaks and glaciers is nothing less than breathtaking, but it improves. Quiet walkers have a good chance of watching chamois at relatively close quarters in this area.

The path is broader now and heads SW in wide curves and soon climbs to a picturesque huddle of huts, **Meyes di Sopra (2518m)** which blends in perfectly with its rock-lichen surroundings.

Not much further up and a final series of ex-glacial 'steps' gives access to the central section of Valle delle Meyes, where your passage will undoubtedly send marmots shrieking and scampering in all directions. After a small lake is a signposted path junction (2615m, 2h10) as you join the wide ex-hunting track in this desolate and unfrequented valley. (See below for the Eaux Rousses extension.) It is worthwhile continuing W up Valle delle Meyes for further exploration. The narrow path crosses moraine and ventures to the foot of small Ghiacciaio di Percià. Eagle sightings are not unusual in these upper reaches. The raptors are said to have perfected the hunting technique of knocking wild animals off their rock crest lookout positions.

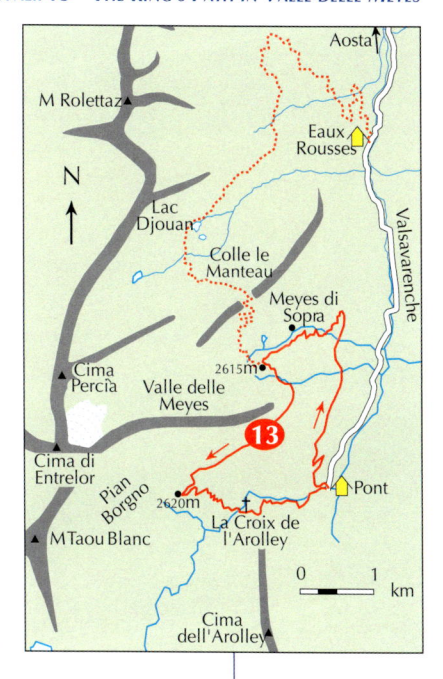

*The old game track in Valle delle Meyes*

## WALK 13 – THE KING'S PATH IN VALLE DELLE MEYES

From the Valle delle Meyes path junction, turn left on n.9 heading first E then S. Gradual descent leads through squelchy boggy flats alongside the stream. Both waymarking and path tend to peter out periodically then reappear. Your aim is to cross the watercourse and rejoin the wide stretch of track visible ahead SE in order to round the rock bastion of the Costa des Aouille – the name probably coming from the word for eagle. Just past the corner is a lookout point par excellence: high over deep U-shaped Valsavarenche is an imposing ridge running S then SW, featuring – from left to right – the Herbetet, Becca di Montandayne, Piccolo and Gran Paradiso, Tresenta, Ciarforon, Becca di Monciair and Denti del Broglio.

The path continues its gradual climb as it enters **Pian Borgno (1h)**, another high-altitude marshy flat soaked by several meltwater streams from higher glacier pockets glimpsed around Mont Taou Blanc (SW, the name refers to the whitish-yellow rock). It is worth checking the rocks above every now and again for chamois. A small tarn precedes a stream crossing on stepping stones. Not far from here, orderly mounds of stones left after pasture-clearing work announce a faded signpost and **path junction (2620m)**.

### Extension: Col del Nivolet (2h)

From the path junction at 2620m after Pian Borgno, the n.2A continues straight on SSW for **Col del Nivolet (2612m)**. (See Walk 12.)

For the descent to Pont, take the left turning (n.3A), decisively downhill. Another excellent easy well-kept path, it winds valleywards between curious dry stone columns-cum-oversized cairns. Flights of stone steps lead quickly to the dirt road at 2485m, a surviving stretch of the Pont–Col del Nivolet road project. You cut straight across it – signposted n.3 for Pont. Continue down to the abandoned huts of Alpe de Turin (2388m), but before actually reaching them, take the unnumbered path off left (ignore n.3A which turns right). Near some cascades it crosses a clearing with profusions of spotted gentians beneath power lines and across a wooden bridge. The main Pont–Col del Nivolet track (n.3) is joined not far from an old wooden cross in a commanding position. A well-used local reference point, **La Croix de l'Arolley** or Croce Arolley **(2310m, 40min)** derives its name from the Arolla pine.

From here the path drops down E in a series of tight zigzags with built-up well-reinforced corners and near a waterfall to the left, enters a larch wood with alpenrose and juniper shrubs. You emerge on the road only a couple of metres from your starting point at **Pont (1960m, 40min)**.

### Extension: Colle le Manteau to Eaux Rousses (3h20)

From the path junction at 2615m in Valle delle Meyes, take a wide track to the right (n.9) heading N. Once on the southern flank of the Costa le Manteau or Mentò, it climbs in easy wide curves, giving you ample time to observe the ibex grazing or at rest among the scattered rocks. The panoramic crest is crossed at **Colle le Manteau (2795m)** and the outlook is spectacular. The track then descending NW was reconstructed in 1964 and is a long easy series of bends. Down in the valley it merges into the AV2 and you turn down right (NE) towards **Lac Djouan (2515m, 1h30)**.

Continue NNE past the old game lodge at Orvieille, then through woods to the hamlet of **Eaux Rousses (1666m, 1h50)**. (See also Stage 6 of the AV2.)

---

**Pont:** Hotel Gran Paradiso tel 0165 95454 www.hotelgparadiso.com; Hotel Genzianella tel 0165 95393 www.genzianella.aosta.it. Small grocery shop and campsite.

## WALK 14
*Vallon di Sort*

| | |
|---|---|
| Time | 4h15 |
| Distance | 9km/5.5 miles |
| Ascent/descent | 840m/840m |
| Grade | 2 |
| Start/finish | Bruil, Rhêmes-Notre-Dame |
| Map | L'Escursionista sheet 3, 1:25,000 |
| Access | Bruil, the main settlement of Rhêmes-Notre-Dame, is served by year-round buses from Aosta. There is ample parking. |

In beautiful Val di Rhêmes, this loop itinerary climbs the little-visited side valley Vallon di Sort before traversing an easy saddle to drop into the vast and more popular Vallon di Entrelor, where it joins the Alta Via 2. Wildlife sightings, chamois and marmots in particular, are almost guaranteed all year round, as well as an excellent range, variety and concentrations of unusual alpine flowers. The curious name Rhêmes, used for both the valley and villages, probably comes from *remma* or *rame*, branch or beam in French, a reference to the valley's old timber industry.

The National Park visitor centre at nearby Chavaney is worth a visit if only for its enormous stuffed lammergeier, or bearded vulture, one of the last specimens from the times when people were paid to shoot them. It is a precious chance to examine this gigantic raptor at close range.

From the church in the small square of **Bruil, Rhêmes-Notre-Dame (1723m)** take the lane cutting through the old houses and E over the torrent. With AV2 waymarking a path leads up off the road, signed for Entrelor/Sort. Past old buildings and up into tree cover, take a left fork at a **1857m junction** (n.9) marked for Col du Sort. ▶ Underfoot are red cowberries, alpenrose and slender martagon lilies. The trouble-free path heads due E and climbs into vast silent Vallon di Sort, in the cover

*The wood is particularly beautiful here, larch mostly but interspersed with Arolla pines and alive with noisy nutcracker birds.*

## GRAN PARADISO – ALTA VIA 2 TREK AND DAY WALKS

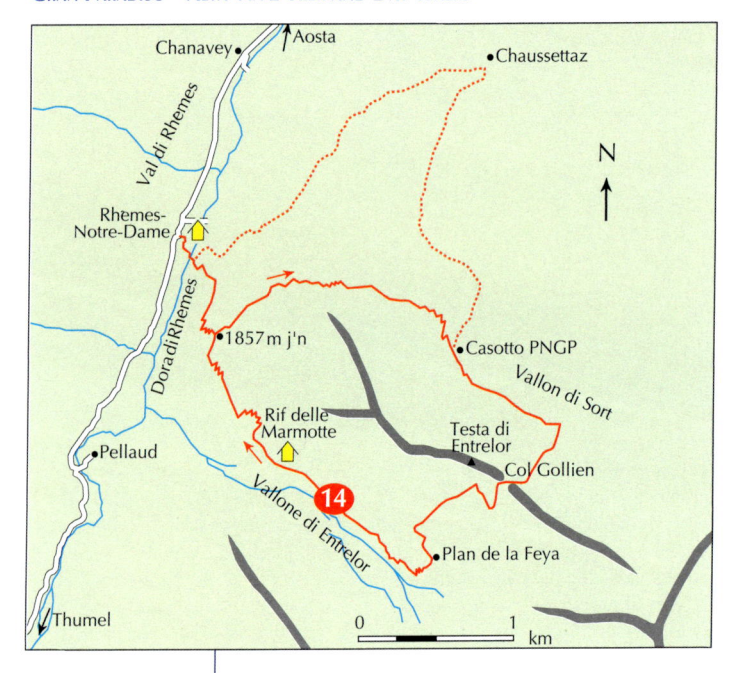

of wood all the way to the lovely position of the **Casotto PNGP (2295m, 1h30**, drinking water). The imposing mass of the Grande Rousse (W) dominates the landscape here but keep scanning the nearby ridges for chamois.

The wide track (now n.7) continues briefly SE towards a stream and marmot colonies. In the vicinity of a large wooden pole keep an eye out for the junction right for Vallone di Entrelor. Climb up now to the ruined huts of Montagna di Sort (2445m). Before turning your back on this upper valley, it is worth a pause to examine the ex-glacial landscape to the east as there are some well-preserved moraine crests.

A fainter path SW climbs over rock marked by the occasional cairn and yellow mark to the ample 2560m saddle **Col Gollien (1h)** that connects the Sort and Entrelor valleys. From here, you have views of Becca

*WALK 14 – VALLON DI SORT*

Tsambellinaz (SSW) and the Rollettaz (NE behind you). Along the crest W from the pass is **Testa di Entrelor (2580m)**, an apparently insignificant grassy-rocky knob but with better views. (Allow 30min return time to visit it.)

From the lowest point of the pass, cross the grassy slopes in the direction of a small cairn where yellow paint pointers indicate a decisive veer right (SSW). The clear path immediately appears and leads down the side valley to cross a stream. After a stretch beneath a rock outcrop and old stone walled enclosure, a brief climb brings you out at the barrel-roofed huts of **Plan de la Feya (2403m, 25min)**.

You have now entered the beautiful **Vallone di Entrelor**. This is a haven for sizeable herds of chamois and ibex, either occupying the head of the valley or grazing or caring for their young on the opposite flanks spread over the vast grassy basins. Wild flowers here come in great quantities, providing spectacular splashes of colour for the impressive backdrop of the Grande Rousse (W over the Val di Rhêmes).

*Grande Rousse*

*GRAN PARADISO – ALTA VIA 2 TREK AND DAY WALKS*

The descent path NW is well trodden and, after a series of wide curves down to the torrent, keeps to its right bank (see also Stage 6 of the AV2). After a turn-off (to nearby Entrelor, 2143m and **Rifugio delle Marmotte**) the verge of the valley is reached and you veer right for the descent through another healthy conifer wood. After a good lookout point for the magnificent Granta Parei (SSW), you eventually drop past the 1857m junction where the ascent route branched off and return to **Bruil, Rhêmes-Notre-Dame (1723m, 1h20)**.

### Alternative
Should late-lying snow block the 2560m pass earlier in the season, a worthwhile round trip at lower altitudes is possible. From the **Casotto PNGP**, head N to contour round (on n.7) past **Chaussettaz (2191m)**, before returning SW on n.8C to Bruil. (Allow 3h30.)

**Bruil:** Chez Lydia tel 0165 936103 www.hotelchezlidia.it; Agriturismo Lo Sabot tel 0165 936150; Rifugio delle Marmotte tel 389 3488785 www.rifugiodellemarmotte.it, sleeps 12, open mid-June to mid-Sept. Some shops.

## WALK 15
*Col Rosset*

| | |
|---|---|
| Time | 6h |
| Distance | 17.5km/10.8 miles |
| Ascent/descent | 570m/1450m |
| Grade | 2–3 |
| Start/finish | Col del Nivolet/Bruil, Rhêmes-Notre-Dame |
| Map | L'Escursionista sheet 3, 1:25,000 |
| Access | Col del Nivolet is served by a shuttle bus to and from Lago Serrù (Suns and public holidays, July to Aug), with extensions to Ceresole Reale. From there a year-round line goes to Pont Canavese and the railway. (See Walk 12 for more details.) Bruil, the main settlement of Rhêmes-Notre-Dame, is connected by bus to Aosta all year round. |

A short stroll above the Col del Nivolet road is the Piani di Rosset plateau – a stunning expanse of lakes amidst breathtaking scenery from the Tre Levanne (SSE) to the Ciarforon to Gran Paradiso line-up (E), with Mont Taou Blanc and massive Punta Basei close by. A full day could easily be spent just exploring this area, within easy reach of the road and refuges below. (See Walk 12 for more information about Col del Nivolet.)

The traverse route described here meanders across this marvellous *altopiano* then climbs to Col Rosset, an ice-free age-old passage to neighbouring Val di Rhêmes. The ensuing descent is the sole section likely to involve any difficulty – a steep detritus-covered flank, a little unstable especially with soft, late-lying snow. The walk is described as a traverse, concluding in Val di Rhêmes, and a return to the start by bus is long-winded. However, a highly rewarding circuit can be made by sleeping at Rifugio Benevolo then returning to Col del Nivolet next day via Col Basei (see Walk 16). An overnight stop at Rifugio Benevolo, a well-run hut, is always pleasant and would also give you the option to join Walk 17 which crosses to Valgrisenche. An added attraction of upper Val di Rhêmes is the spectacular Granta Parei peak.

*Gran Paradiso – Alta Via 2 Trek and Day Walks*

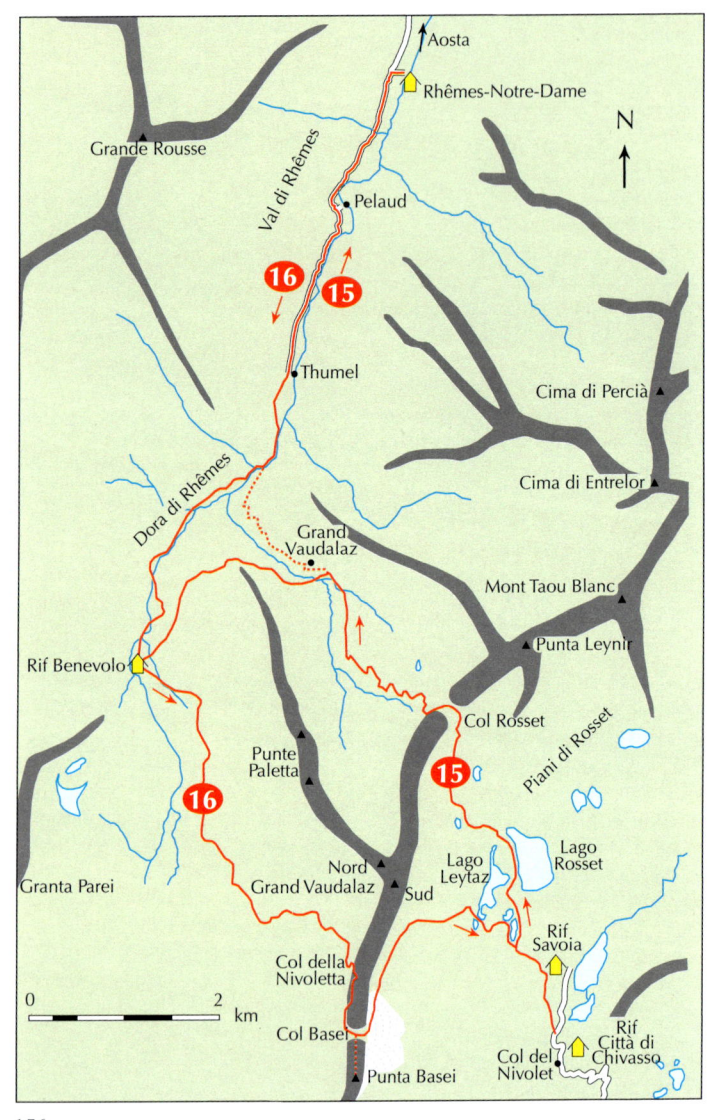

156

## WALK 15 – COL ROSSET

Below the southern side of the **Col del Nivolet** pass **(2612m)**, on the roadside a tad below Rifugio Città di Chivasso, path n.3C turns up left. Climbing NNW over a rise, its way over grassy terrain is marked by yellow arrows. The route leads up onto the vast pasture plateau, **Piani di Rosset**, and between the two major lakes, Lago Rosset and Lago Leytaz, the outlook inspiring to say the least. If you start out from **Rifugio Savoia** head uphill on the popular path for Col Leynir but only as far as Alpage Riva (2590m) with its flowing drinking fountains, then branch left (WSW) to join up with the main route.

A steady but short-lived ascent begins among thick clumps of edelweiss, proceeding along a wide, shiny corridor of mica-schists. The characteristic flowers include brilliant King of the Alps forget-me-not, and a yellow variety of mustard flower similar to a dwarf wallflower. Snow lies in depressions around the path for extended periods and chamois seem to enjoy lazing in it. Several more small lakes (Laghi Chanavey) lie along the way to the base of an escarpment. Now the final 150m uphill is a series of tight and exacting zigzags. Multicoloured rock bands of dark grey-brown, greenstone and pink-tinged limestone are crossed.

**Col Rosset (3023m, 2h)** is quite something, with generous views in all directions. However, an even better view can be had up the clear path right (NE) to the trig point. Looking back, even with the Gran Paradiso out of sight, Tresenta is ESE then Ciarforon, as well as Col del Nivolet with its magnificent backdrop. On the other side, Val di Rhêmes features lower but distinct, light-coloured Granta Parei (WSW) and the crest with Punta Tsantelèynaz (SW), as well as underlying glaciers and continuous moraines. (This path – for expert walkers only – leads on to the summit of Punta Leynir (3235m), meaning 'black lake'.)

For the descent WNW, path n.13A disappears beneath your boots down the initially steep scree-earth slope. Tricky and a little exposed and guided by occasional yellow markings, it embarks on a wide curve left, then zigzags. The going soon becomes a little easier on

*Great views en route to Col Rosset*

## WALK 15 – COL ROSSET

the knees as you return to stable grassed terrain. Amidst flowers and marmots the path veers N, keeping to the right side of Vallon de Grand Vaudalaz and its eponymous torrent, and heads for the old farm buildings of **Grand Vaudalaz (2338m, 1h10)**. Just before reaching them, after a side stream crossing marked by yellow arrows, your narrow path (n.13A) branches left to cross the torrent. (At this point you could carry straight on to exit to Bruil directly, see below.)

Near the torrent crossing you will see 'R Benevolo 40min' painted on a rock, but it will take a little longer. The path climbs diagonally W across mixed rock flows. The dry hillside is alive with grasshoppers and the scree is thick with the large plants of the dull pink-violet felted adenostyle flowers. Continuing up the hillside you climb to a shoulder at 2417m and are rewarded by the wonderful spectacle of light-coloured peaks and ice that crown the head of the **Val di Rhêmes**, in addition to the almost aerial view of the valley floor to the north.

Over rolling pasture and hillocks now, guided by propped-up stones and small cairns, you proceed SW to the refuge, visible ahead on an outcrop. You'll probably lose sight of the path as the cattle, which belong to nearby Alpe Lavassey, usually manage to obliterate it, but waymarking is frequently renewed. If you don't manage to come out on the 4-wheel drive track just below the refuge, wander over the hillside until you spot a convenient stock descent route.

**Rifugio Benevolo (2285m, 50min)**, named after an entomologist from Torino (Turin), is a hospitable old-style if smallish refuge run by qualified staff who know the area like the back of their hand and score high on catering. A regular diner is the sleek fox who drops in after dark for scraps. ▸

When the time comes to point your boots valleywards, ignore the jeep track and cut down the path behind the refuge building. After touching on the track several times, you actually join it at a bridge over the Dora di Rhêmes torrent, and stick with it briefly to a showering cascade. A marked path soon branches off

If you have time to spare, take the easy path leading to the beautiful upper valley to the source of the Dora di Rhêmes torrent beneath several glaciers.

to the right, and leads through delightful landscape with shrubs and plenty of flowers on the banks of the torrent. At the settlement of **Thumel (1879m, 1h10)**, you meet the vehicle track and then come to a car park.

The final leg is 4km along a road through the picturesque hamlet of **Pelaud** to the village of **Bruil, Rhêmes-Notre-Dame (1723m, 50min)** with its hotels, shops and bus stop.

### Variation: Exit to Bruil from Grand Vaudalaz (2h20)

This handy exit takes you directly to the floor of **Val di Rhêmes**. A little further on from the Rifugio Benevolo turn-off are the derelict huts of **Grand Vaudalaz (2338m)**. Soon path n.12 exits the Vallon de Grand Vaudalaz and continues NW down the steep flank to cross the **Dora di Rhêmes**, terminating at the farm settlement of **Thumel (1879m)**. Nearby is a car park and start of the road. From here it is 4km to **Bruil, Rhêmes-Notre-Dame (1723m, 50min)**.

---

**Col del Nivolet:** Rifugio Città di Chivasso tel 0124 953150 http://rifugiochivasso.altervista.org, CAI, sleeps 44, open late June to late Sept; Rifugio Savoia tel 0165 94141 www.rifugiosavoia.com, sleeps 60, open 15 June to 30 Sept
Rifugio Benevolo tel 0165 936143 www.rifugiobenevelo.com, CAI, sleeps 62, open mid-June to mid-Sept
**Bruil:** Chez Lydia tel 0165 936103 www.hotelchezlidia.it; Agriturismo Lo Sabot tel 0165 936150. Some shops.

## WALK 16
*Punta Basei*

| | |
|---|---|
| **Time** | 7h |
| **Distance** | 18.7km/11.6 miles |
| **Ascent/descent** | 1550m/660m |
| **Grade** | 3 |
| **Start/finish** | Bruil, Rhêmes-Notre-Dame/Col del Nivolet |
| **Map** | L'Escursionista sheet 3, 1:25,000 |
| **Access** | Bruil, the main settlement of Rhêmes-Notre-Dame, has year-round buses to Aosta. Col del Nivolet is served by a shuttle bus to and from Lago Serrù (Suns and public holidays, early July to end Aug), with extensions to Ceresole Reale. From there a year-round line goes as far as Pont Canavese and the railway. (See Walk 12 for more details.) |

This is another traverse connecting the splendid upper Val di Rhêmes with the beautiful lake-filled Nivolet *altopiano*. Unlike the more straightforward routes – Walk 15, and Stage 7 of Alta Via 2 – this one climbs to two dizzy cols with panoramic views above 3100m. The ridge in between is exposed to the elements and the loose terrain on both sides demands extra attention. Snow and sometimes ice are to be reckoned with at the start and end of the season and gaiters may come in useful. The best time to go is generally August to early September but that will vary a little from year to year.

A rewarding optional ascent to the summit of Punta Basei is included here, but only for those with a sure foot along with some experience on icy terrain. The peak is popular from the Col del Nivolet side as it is closer, and both cols make rewarding day trips from their respective valleys.

The best way to tackle the route as described here is to stay overnight at Rifugio Benevolo, so as to break up the substantial ascent. This is a well-run hut that feeds its guests well.

From the square in the village of **Bruil, Rhêmes-Notre-Dame (1723m)** take the 4km asphalt road S up to the parking area at the farming settlement of **Thumel**

For map see Walk 15

**(1879m)**. See Walk 17 for the description of the clearly marked path that climbs from here to bustling old-style **Rifugio Benevolo (2285m, 2h30)**. Don't expect more than basic washing facilities but meals come in filling portions.

Near the building a clutch of yellow signposts indicates n.13B for Col Nivoletta. ◄ Climbing gently left (SSE) it passes a fascinating example of the livestock stalls built into the natural slope of the land so as to conserve heat and reduce damage in case of avalanches. Parallel to the valley floor it proceeds above the watercourse, well beneath Punte Paletta. At just over 2400m the path bears SE and launches into a steady ascent, cutting across myriad tiny streams from glaciers high above. Views around the head of Val di Rhêmes improve with every step – the magnificent light limestone Granta Parei (W), then pyramidal Punta Tsantelèynaz (WSW) and a sequence of smaller graceful peaks including Roc du Fond and Roc Basagne over the diminishing glaciers (S). Walkers may surprise chamois at pasture on flowered flats in the shade of the Grand Vaudalaz points. Above the 2700m mark shiny, slaty-looking schists are underfoot while

**Note:** there is often confusion between the road pass Col del Nivolet and walkers-only Col della Nivoletta. Different maps use different spellings, but the main distinguishing feature is the word Nivolet or Nivoletta.

*The Granta Parei in upper Val di Rhêmes*

## WALK 16 – PUNTA BASEI

the sparse vegetation features the tough yellowish felted genepi flowers, beloved by the local people for making their famous spirit.

The going is steep and tiring and a final leg swings from NE to SE, eventually bringing you out at the cairn on airy **Col della Nivoletta (3130m, 2h30)**. The breathtaking crest offers views of Gran Paradiso (ENE), Ciarforon (E), the Levanne line-up (SE) and then the lakes nestling in the numerous depressions around Col del Nivolet, where the road is visible far below.

To reach southernmost Col Basei follow the loose debris crest, ascending briefly at first. Special care is needed as there are uncertain and exposed stretches above precipitous gullies, which require short detours. You finally reach **Col Basei (3176m, 30min)**, at the foot of Punta Basei (straight up the crest S, looking for all the world like a square castle).

*Crossing a snowfield en route to Punta Basei*

### Optional ascent to Punta Basei (1h return time)
The ascent to the summit is reserved for walkers with some climbing experience as the final leg usually

involves ice and rock passages, requiring the appropriate equipment (ice pick and crampons). From the col the rounded crest is followed S to where an upper section of Ghiacciaio Basei is encountered. After a rock climb aided by fixed cable, it is not far to the metal cross on the spectacular **Punta Basei (3338m)**.

Return carefully the same way to **Col Basei**.

From **Col Basei** the way down traverses a long section of the Ghiacciaio Basei. By midsummer it is usually a snow field. Take the well-trodden diagonal piste due N in gradual descent. When you leave the glacier and reach loose rubble-earth terrain, the occasional cairn guides you in a curve around NE and onto a clearer path. Here red waymarking also becomes apparent. A rock spur is reached with a bird's-eye view over the Piani di Rosset and its lakes and then tight zigzags drop down a steep edelweiss-studded flank to the southern end of **Lago Leytaz (2701m)**.

The path heads E over hillocks, and joins wider n.3C. Yellow arrows point you SSE past more small lakes then follow an ample curve to cross a cascading torrent. At an unmarked junction keep left for modest **Rifugio Savoia (2532m)**. Otherwise the right branch will bring you out on the roadside. Cut over SE for the alpine-style **Rifugio Città di Chivasso (2604m)**. The actual road pass, **Col del Nivolet (2612m, 1h30)**, is a little further uphill.

---

**Col del Nivolet:** Rifugio Città di Chivasso tel 0124 953150 http://rifugiochivasso.altervista.org, CAI, sleeps 44, open late June to late Sept;
Rifugio Savoia tel 0165 94141 www.rifugiosavoia.com, sleeps 60, open 15 June to 30 Sept;
Rifugio Benevolo tel 0165 936143 www.rifugiobenevelo.com, CAI, sleeps 62, open mid-June to mid-Sept

## WALK 17
### Becca della Traversière

| | |
|---|---|
| Time | 11h15 |
| Distance | 33km/20.5 miles |
| Ascent/descent | 1610m/1670m |
| Grade | 3 |
| Start/finish | Bruil, Rhêmes-Notre-Dame/Valgrisenche |
| Map | L'Escursionista sheet 3, 1:25,000 |
| Access | Bruil, the main settlement of Rhêmes-Notre-Dame, and Valgrisenche can be reached by year-round bus from Aosta. |

This is a hard walk to beat. Starting out in beautiful Val di Rhêmes, just outside the western confines of the Gran Paradiso Park, it takes in a spectacular ice-free walkers' peak before following a glacier edge down into rugged Valgrisenche. With the exception of the opening and closing stretches, Thumel to Rifugio Benevolo and Rifugio Bezzi to Uselères, which are popular with day visitors due to the refuges, these paths do not see many walkers. Once away from the huts, you find yourself in wild desolate valleys edged with inspiring and sobering seas of ice.

The summit section is quite exceptional – Becca della Traversière on the Italian-French border only recently became accessible for walkers because of the ongoing retreat of ice on both sides of the Col Bassac Déré pass. A surprisingly good path for that altitude, it leads to a dizzy perch, requiring a good head for heights, with 360° views high over the Alps.

Mid to late summer is the best time to go as snow cover should be at a manageable minimum, although gaiters are always a good idea. Overall the walk is of average difficulty, but in view of the height gain and timing, it is advisable to plan on overnighting at a refuge.

Wonderful day walks for all walkers are feasible in both valleys as the lower zones described are covered by easy paths. Rifugio Benevolo and Rifugio Bezzi both score well on hospitality and make great bases for exploring their respective areas. You can drive as far as Thumel in Val di Rhêmes, or Uselères in Valgrisenche, to reduce access times. For instance,

Thumel–Rifugio Benevolo–Lago Goletta and return, should only be a total of 5h.
**Note:** Valgrisenche is the name both for the valley and its principal village.

From the square at **Bruil, Rhêmes-Notre-Dame (1723m)** leave the village by way of the narrowing surfaced road S. Further on is the picturesque hamlet of Pelaud (1811m) and higher up a large parking area as unauthorised traffic can proceed no further. The active, if small, farming community of **Thumel (1879m)** follows. Where the jeep track curves right a wide path goes straight ahead S. Clearly signposted for Rifugio Benevolo, it is also referred to as the 'Pison' route, possibly from the name of a local avalanche.

The delightful, old, paved path follows the right bank of the Dora di Rhêmes torrent most of the way, and is ablaze with unusual flowers such as willow gentians and pink orchids. There are several lovely cascades and the backdrop is provided by the unmistakable towering Granta Parei massif (S). The jeep track is joined in

*Rifugio Benevolo*

*WALK 17 – BECCA DELLA TRAVERSIÈRE*

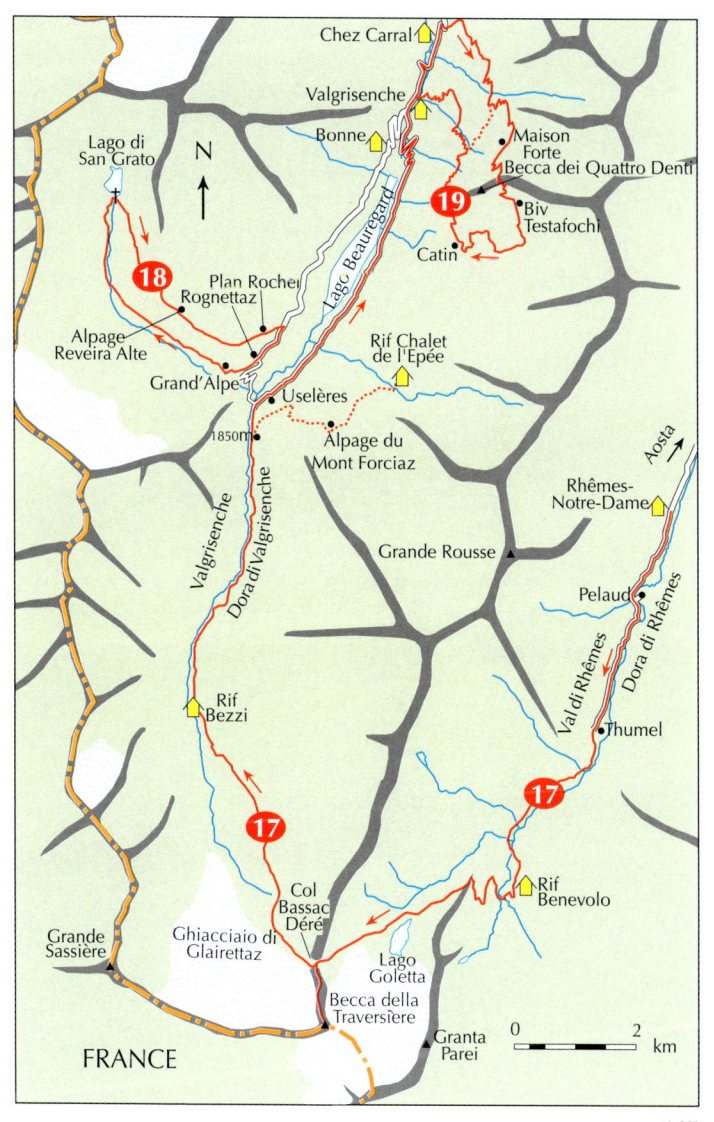

*GRAN PARADISO – ALTA VIA 2 TREK AND DAY WALKS*

the vicinity of a waterfall that will soak slow passers-by. After the nearby bridge the path cuts up a steep flank and finally clambers up to the natural platform hosting **Rifugio Benevolo (2285m, 2h30)**. As far as facilities go, the hut has been modernised. Moreover, the meals come in generous portions and leftovers sometimes go to the fox which hangs around in the hope of scraps after dinner. In the early morning the Granta Parei, whose name comes from 'grande parete', great wall, is at its best, illuminated to perfection.

From the hut follow waymarking (n.13D) down to the stone bridge across the torrent. The easy path climbs diagonally NNW to the old farm buildings of Sotses or Sauches (2313m), depending on which map you have, then sharp left (S). You pass a turn-off for the Granta Parei lake and keep right up the steep zigzags to the crest where there are magnificent views E to the Gran Paradiso. This leads SW into the stone desert plateau, Comba di Golettaz, following cairns along the left bank of the torrent. Below the triangular point of the Granta Parei (S), the wrinkled surface of the Ghiacciaio di Golettaz forms the uppermost banks of grey **Lago**

*Lago Goletta and Granta Parei*

168

## WALK 17 – BECCA DELLA TRAVERSIÈRE

**Goletta (2699m)**. This is an unworldy spot, frequented solely by enormous grey ravens.

Stepping stones cross the lake outlet and the path continues up the right side of the valley. Snow cover lasts long into the summer in these high reaches, but plenty of yellow waymarking should be visible. You climb steadily, alternating debris and snow. The flowers are surprisingly abundant in midsummer, and the varied colourful rocks, including limestone, host blue Mount Cenis bellflowers, white alpine mouse-ear and yellow daisies – an irresistible attraction for butterflies. The final stretch to the pass crosses a steep, permanent snow field, necessitating a little extra care. You eventually step out at the narrow saddle of **Col Bassac Déré (3082m, 3h)**, a breathtaking spot. A massive expanse of ice, Ghiacciaio di Glairettaz, completely fills the next valley and above it is immense dark Grande Sassière (W). Back E the line-up extends from the Gran Paradiso to the Grivola (NE).

### Ascent to Becca della Traversière (1h return) ▶

From **Col Bassac Déré** take the unnumbered path left (due S) and around to a saddle where there may be ibex. A

**Note:** This ascent is straightforward in good conditions but on the way down from the peak the path will feel more exposed. It is recommended for experienced walkers only.

*Climbing to Becca della Traversière high above Lago Goletta*

clear path winds up the crest to the top of **Becca della Traversière (3337m)**, the edge of Italy, where you'll encounter mountaineers who have climbed up over rock and ice from the French side. It is simply stunning. Seas of white extend in all directions, and over them, with any luck, you will be rewarded by the sight of Mont Blanc (NNW) and the Matterhorn (NW), to mention a few, in addition to the lovely peaks WSW beyond Val d'Isère on the French side. Take the descent slowly the same way back to **Col Bassac Déré**.

The narrow dirt path (n.12C) drops right (W) on loose terrain and makes its way towards the edge of the glacier, then skirting above it to head N. The descent is gradual and problem-free, accompanied by the sight of distant Mont Blanc, not to mention the grandiose ridge to the W. Endless tongues of snow are crossed below Punta Bassac Déré then Punta Bassac Sud in a desolate, silent, high-altitude landscape, morainic for the most part. A rainbow of rocks is underfoot – greens, purples and greys – supporting different flowers.

After a good hour the valley narrows and concertina crevasses on the vast body of ice announce a change of gradient in the form of a sudden drop. The path similarly reaches the edge of an escarpment, still at around 2850m, and grassy terrain at last. The refuge is visible below now, while N is the Testa del Ruitor with Mont Chateau Blanc to its right. The path drops quickly (NNW), sometimes on loose debris, possibly snow-covered. The terrain is thickly flowered and a couple of side torrents are crossed or forded. Some powerful waterfalls drop off to the left.

You eventually reach the welcoming **Rifugio Bezzi (2284m, 2h)**, set among emerald pastures. The smaller wing of the hut dates back to the 1930s but the refuge now boasts a spacious brand new section with all mod cons. Solar-heated showers are free of charge. You are well looked after and well fed here, and the menu may feature local specialities such as the Valle d'Aosta rice dish 'risotto alla valdostana'.

## WALK 17 – BECCA DELLA TRAVERSIÈRE

*Enjoying a meal at Rifugio Bezzi*

Past the hut's mechanised cableway, path n.12 heads downhill due N on the right side of the watercourse Dora di Valgrisenche. The valley opens up considerably and in the vicinity of ruined huts (Alpage Sasse de Savoie, 2036m) overgrown by masses of rosebay willowherb, a wide motorable track is reached, in the vicinity of the refuge's cableway.

Further on is a key junction at 1850m – the link for walkers intending to pick up Alta Via 2, Stage 8 (see below). Go straight ahead to the abandoned hamlet of **Uselères (1785m, 1h15)** and a parking area. There is also a summer eatery, where you can enjoy a tasty meal, snack or just a drink while eavesdropping on the gossip, in the 'unintelligible' dialect-patois of local shepherds.

The remaining 6km or so to Valgrisenche are along the narrow road above the eastern (right) edge of Lago Beauregard. After six villages were flooded in the 1950s, along with this central section of Valgrisenche, the dam revealed itself unsafe and so the lake had to be drained to the present low level. Although the road is surfaced, this stretch is not regularly maintained so drivers tend to use the higher route on the opposite bank. At the end of the dam the road curves downwards. to **Valgrisenche (1664m, 1h30)**.

### Detour to Rifugio Chalet de l'Epée (1h30)
Turn right at the 1850m junction for the 4-wheel drive track NE uphill. Shortly, break off right (SE), signposted 'Rifugio Chalet de l'Epée' (continuing along the road takes 10min more). Path n.9A winds up through beautiful wood with some magnificent monumental larch trees sheltering pale pink alpenrose and concentrations of bilberry shrubs loaded with juicy fruit in midsummer. In the openings between, the Gran Becca du Mont appears NW on the border with France, as well as Col du Mont pass (WNW).

The pretty pasture basin occupied by **Alpage du Mont Forciaz (2180m)** is reached, beneath the shimmering pocket glaciers of the Grande Rousse (SE). Make your way across the marshy terrain and past the buildings, soon breaking off the farm lane to climb NNE to cut diagonally across the dry hillside. This emerges in a rocky basin ablaze with alpenrose. The vehicle track is soon rejoined for the last leg to family-run **Rifugio Chalet de l'Epée (2370m)**.

---

Rifugio Benevolo tel 0165 936143 www.rifugiobenevolo.com, CAI, sleeps 62, open mid-June to mid-Sept; Rifugio Bezzi tel 0165 97129 www.rifugiobezzi.com, private but applies CAI rates, sleeps 105, open mid-June to mid-Sept

## WALK 18
*Legendary San Grato*

| | |
|---|---|
| **Time** | 3h45 |
| **Distance** | 9.7km/6 miles |
| **Ascent/descent** | 515m/515m |
| **Grade** | 2 |
| **Start/finish** | Rognettaz parking area |
| **Map** | L'Escursionista sheet 3, 1:25,000 |
| **Access** | Valgrisenche is served by year-round buses from Aosta. However, the walk start is a further 6km and 350m uphill by surfaced road. If on foot either try hitching a lift or be prepared to add 3h (return time) to the walk total. |

A homage to the intriguing figure of San Grato, 5th-century bishop of Aosta and patron saint, combined with an easy pastoral walk in upper Valgrisenche to the lake and chapel named after him. Threatened with persecution in his native Sparta, Grato fled to Rome but learnt from divine messengers that his mission was to evangelise the mountainous area of Aosta. A later vision sent him to the Holy Land for the head of John the Baptist, decapitated by Herod Antipas to reward Salome for her dancing. The ensuing episode is another legend in itself – the miraculous location by an angel of the relic in a deep pit. Back in Rome, when the time came to present the precious trophy to the Pope, only the skull came away leaving the jawbone in the hand of Grato! Carried to Aosta, it is still kept in the Cathedral Treasury in an ornate 15th-century reliquary.

The remains of the saint himself are similarly treasured. They have long been attributed with miraculous powers and fragments were in great demand. In the late 14th century they were even stolen, but recovered in haste by a determined group of builders from Fontainemore in Valle di Gressoney. During their return journey over alpine passes en route to Aosta, they rested awhile on the shores of what is now known as Lago di San Grato and a tiny chapel was erected on the spot in remembrance. In modern-day Valgrisenche 5 September is celebrated as 'Lo Patron de Sen Grat', with a procession to the lake and chapel, while 5 August sees another procession in honour of Our Lady of the Snows.

Valgrisenche – the name for both the valley and the major settlement – is also well known for its traditional woven woollen fabric, on display at the locally run cooperative workshop which uses enormous looms. The unusual goat battles (late September) are an added attraction, along with the Battailles des Reines with cows. The valley's lake, Lago di Beauregard, was created in the 1950s, with the flooding of six villages in the name of hydro-electricity. It is deliberately maintained at a low level for safety reasons by the Electricity Commission, due to construction errors.

The walk is rather lengthy if you start out on foot from Valgrisenche, although a recommended overnight stay at hospitable Hotel Perret at Bonne (1810m) shortens it a tad. While there is no difficulty in normal conditions, remember that the valley housing the lake tends to accumulate snow which can last well into summer, covering the stream, bridge and path on the upper section. It is therefore more suitable for midsummer, unless you are prepared for snow walking.

For map see Walk 17

From the parking area at **Rognettaz (1950m)** a stroll uphill brings you to a large old-style summer dairy farm, **Grand'Alpe (1998m)** at the opening of Vallon Saint Grat. The wide track (n.14) continues NW to climb almost imperceptibly along the N flank of this ample pasture valley. Summer is proclaimed by expanses of yellow and white alpine pasque flowers, purple orchids and banks of pink alpenrose shrubs. Romping marmots add the finishing touch.

High above the torrent stand the long low stone stalls of Alpe Reveira Basse (2153m). Here the track narrows and soon a signpost announces the Lago di San Grato fork to the right. (Path n.13 continues W down to a bridge before innumerable twists and turns in ascent past an ex-barracks to the historical Col du Mont (2639m) pass and France – a worthwhile 1h45. ◀ ) As you proceed N up this side valley, Gran Becca du Mont is the peak facing you NW with Becca du Lac due N. You come to a gushing torrent near the base of a waterfall and cross to the left bank by way of a bridge – if it has not

Long used by the Gauls, the pass also witnessed the heroic stand by Piemonte soldiers against French invasion attempts in the 1790s.

## WALK 18 – LEGENDARY SAN GRATO

been washed away again. Alternating gentle climbs and flatter stretches, the path moves up to cut the final steepish flank of this lower basin. As the terrain is unstable and snow often lies late here, expect soft crumbly sections of path, maybe necessitating a few detours.

The minuscule chapel shrine to San Grato, lovingly restored, stands slightly below **Lago di San Grato (2462m, 2h15)** and its grandiose setting. High in the NNE corner of its rocky amphitheatre is Testa del Ruitor, on the edge of the massive glacier, while the Becca du Lac dominates in the NNW.

Take the narrow concreted passageway across the lake's outlet, and follow the clear path (n.14A) that cuts the steep mountainside SE, contouring high above the valley climbed previously. At the junctions keep to the lower (right) branch. Gentle descent on this panoramic path leads to **Alpage Reveira Alte (2324m)**. Wild flowers abound on this pasture in summer. From this vantage point you can see SE to the graceful line-up of mountains featuring Grande Rousse, then S to the narrow ridge that constitutes the western border of upper Valgrisenche. Leave n.14A and bear right (SE) on the clear path for **Plan**

*Gran Becca du Mont dominates the path for Lago San Grato*

# Gran Paradiso – Alta Via 2 Trek and Day Walks

*Late-lying snow below Lago di San Grato*

**Rocher**, where it is possible to cut down to the road not far from the **Rognettaz** parking area (1950m, 1h30).

**Valgrisenche**: Ostello Le Vieux Quartier tel 0165 974101 www.levieux quartier.com

# WALK 19
## Becca dei Quattro Denti

| | |
|---|---|
| Time | 5h30 |
| Distance | 14km/8.6 miles |
| Ascent/descent | 1210m/1210m |
| Grade | 2–3 |
| Start/finish | Valgrisenche |
| Map | L'Escursionista sheet 3, 1:25,000 |
| Access | Valgrisenche has year-round buses from Aosta. |

This marvellous circuit in Valgrisenche has as its destination the modest Becca dei Quattro Denti. So named for the 'four teeth' of rock along its crest, it is a surprisingly good viewpoint over the multitude of peaks in upper Valgrisenche. An interesting variety of landscapes is covered on the way up, from tranquil conifer woods to thickly flowered meadows and stony slopes. En route are ruins of a historical fort and a series of old stone wall fortifications testifying to the valley's preparations when faced with an imminent French invasion in the 1790s – the time of Napoleon's Second Italian Campaign.

No particular difficulties are involved, but a little extra attention is needed for waymarking in several spots. The very top section covers unstable terrain and can be avoided if desired. Early walkers should expect snow on the final ascent to Bivacco Testafochi, a rudimentary yet superbly positioned hut.

From the township of **Valgrisenche (1664m)**, go N down the main road and shortcut through to Gerbelle over the river, then keep on for the hamlet of **Chez Carral** and welcoming guesthouse Maison des Myrtilles. Soon after a bend in the road is a yellow signpost for Becca dei Quattro Denti and Alta Via 2. Proceeding on through fields, clear path n.5 is walled-in at first. At the torrent, keep to the right bank. Through mixed conifer woods

For map see Walk 17

you head up through pasture clearings and abandoned huts. Massive snowcapped Grande Sassière is upvalley SSW.

The path bears right (SSE) to nearby Verconey damon huts (1980m) and a modest ski lift. Follow the wide track, then leave the AV2 at old fortifications. Stick to the track, which winds and plods steadily up to the low but extensive walls of stone fort **Maison Forte (2399m, 2h)**. Constructed in 1795 when skirmishes were already regular occurrences between the French and Piemonte soldiers at Col du Mont over to the W, it was a strategic part of the extensive design of Valgrisenche's fortifications. The position, naturally, offers wide-ranging views. The sharp 'teeth' of the Becca dei Quattro Denti can be identified up on the ridge (S). Continue on past what's left of Alp. Maison Forte, which is easy to miss. You drop briefly to the edge of a basin. Keep to its left side on the mule track (now path n.6) that makes its way up in countless wide zigzags that betray its military origin.

*Valgrisenche*

## WALK 19 – BECCA DEI QUATTRO DENTI

On **Becca dei Quattro Denti (2618m, 1h)** are remains of more 18th-century fortifications, not to mention marvellous views. Included are Testa del Ruitor (WNW) and M. Chateau Blanc (NW).

From here it is possible to follow an initially steep descent path (n.7A), a variant return, or turn E on the narrow ridge where the terrain is crumbly and a sure foot needed. This leads to **Bivacco Testafochi (2695m, 15min)**, a spartan hut that belongs to the Forestry Commission; emergency shelter only. Towering over a vast pasture amphitheatre, with its old summer farms, is pointed Becca di Tey (SSE), then S is triangular Grande Rousse.

A clear if narrow path (n.6) cuts S diagonally down the slope amidst extraordinary numbers of pasque flowers. At the stream you turn right to join a vehicle track in easy descent. (The alternative path from the crest joins up at the next bend.) Further down is **Catin (2302m, 1h)**, a picturesque scattering of buildings and an AV2 junction. Turn right through a veritable botanic garden dominated by purple orchids, for delightful contouring around the midriff of Becca dei Quattro Denti. The way narrows and drops. At the 2100m mark a narrow precipitious path (n.6) plunges left to **Valgrisenche (1664m, 1h15)**. ▶

As an **alternative** if you wish to return directly to Chez Carral, continue N on AV2 to rejoin the ascent route at the fortifications on the track, and allow an extra 30min.

**Chez Carral:** Maison des Myrtilles tel 0165 97118

*Gran Paradiso – Alta Via 2 Trek and Day Walks*

# WALK 20
## The Royal Track to Ceresole Reale

| | |
|---|---|
| Time | 8h |
| Distance | 24km/14.9 miles |
| Ascent/descent | 910m/1920m |
| Grade | 2–3 |
| Start/finish | Col del Nivolet/Ceresole Reale |
| Map | L'Escursionista sheet 14, 1:25,000 |
| Access | See Walk 12 for Col del Nivolet. Ceresole Reale is served by year-round bus to the railhead of Pont Canavese. |

A marvellous panoramic route of average difficulty along the most extensive surviving lengths of the original mule-track constructed for the royal hunting parties in the mid-1800s. You should enjoy sweeping views and adventurous walking in desolate landscapes with very few other human beings but plenty of wild animals. This is probably one of the best walks in this guide.

Following a lengthy initial stage, high up with superb views, the first pass, Colle della Terra, marks the entry into more desolate inner valleys below towering peaks. You skirt around Cima di Courmaon and descend upper Vallon del Roc touching on a series of picturesque but abandoned shepherds' huts – sizeable clusters of admirable dry stone work. The last leg drops through woodland on the northern flank of Valle dell'Orco.

More manageable chunks of the walk are easily bitten off and shorter round walks possible – for instance descending to Mua, not far from Ceresole Reale, after Lago Lillet. Alternatively, this walk can be spread over two days with an overnight stay in Bivacco Ettore e Margherita Giraudo (sometimes referred to as Bivacco Margherita or Bivacco Giraudo). This involves a brief detour off the main path and you will need sleeping and cooking gear, not to mention food. The tiny hut has six bunk beds and meltwater can be found nearby. An extention via Vallon del Roc to Noasca is also feasible.

**Note**: As the complete itinerary is very long, an early start is essential and extra time should be allowed for unclear waymarking, collapsed stretches of path and snow cover, including a gently sloping permanent

*WALK 20 – THE ROYAL TRACK TO CERESOLE REALE*

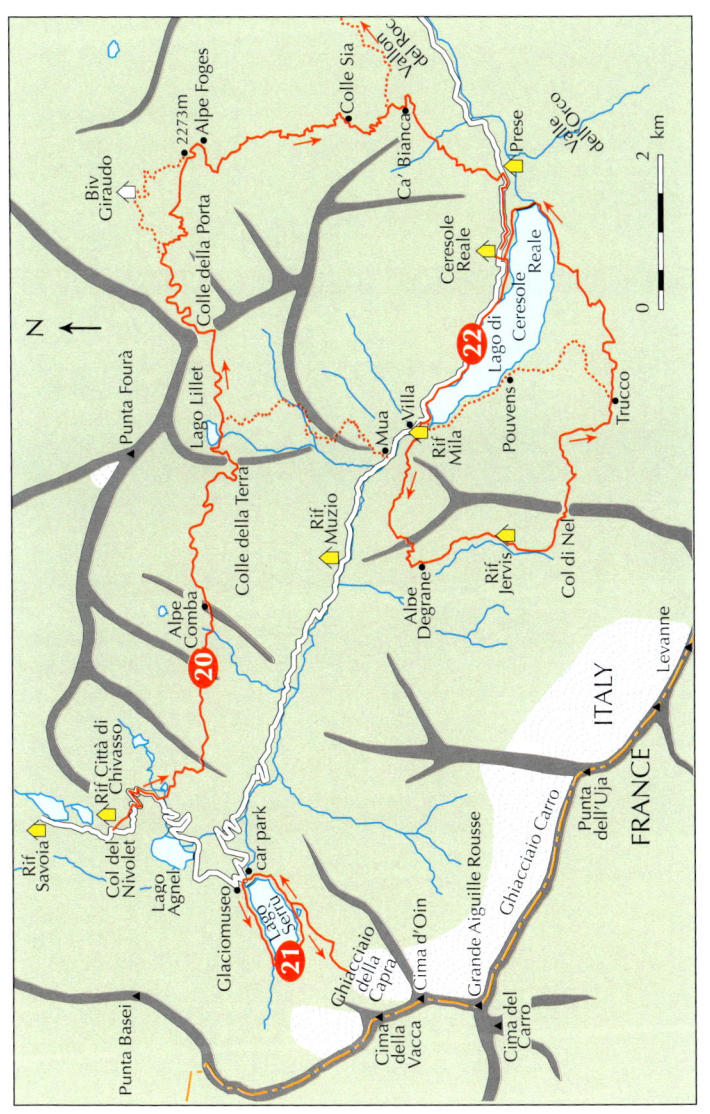

snow field in the proximity of Colle della Porta where gaiters can be handy. The helpful custodian at Rifugio Città di Chivasso knows the area well, should you require more information before starting out. It is inadvisable to set out on the route in uncertain weather. Not to be underestimated are the mist and low cloud which make orientation decidedly difficult, and which are typical of these valleys.

## WEATHER FAIRIES: GOOD & BAD!

The storms in the area are reputedly caused by wind imps letting loose cloud masses at their will from strategic passes, then setting off thunder and lightning with their clashes. The good news is that the whereabouts of Col del Nivolet have long been renowned for the presence of the ephemeral White Dames, white-robed creatures who flit across steep mountainsides and through avalanches to pluck out unfortunate mountaineers.

From **Col del Nivolet (2612m)** take the old game track starting in the vicinity of Rifugio Città di Chivasso. It leads SE past a small lake and winds down to the road, its wide curves supported by interesting built-up stonework. Views are breathtaking as you are high above the dammed Agnel and Serrù lakes, looking over upper Valle dell'Orco to the crest with Cima del Carro (WSW), Punta dell'Uja (S), then the Levanne pyramids (SSE), interspersed with minor ice fields.

On the roadside near an unnamed lake at 2461m, a wooden signpost marks the start of the wide track (n.550). Bearing SE at first it rounds Costa della Civetta before going due E, practically parallel to the valley floor. This long panoramic level stretch with tidy stone borders is in good condition and it is easy to imagine the processions of horses bearing privileged hunters and their entourages. The watercourses crossed run down from isolated lakes scattered over a vast ex-glacial area out of sight above, on the southern flanks of the crest linking Punta Violetta and Punta Fourà (so named for a 'hole' in its crest, visible from afar).

## WALK 20 – THE ROYAL TRACK TO CERESOLE REALE

After a second group of old stone huts **Alpe Comba (2549m)** (where a signed path drops to Chiapili di Sopra), the track curves left to cross a watercourse. It then starts its steady climb towards the first pass. ▶ Loose rock and earth prevail, providing meagre yet still attractive pasture for the chamois observable here, along with the ibex. A wooden signpost marks **Colle della Terra (2911m, 2h30)**. The wide saddle separates insignificant Punta Rocchetta (S) and the crest that descends from Mare Percia (NE), with its 'pierced' peak. The landscape changes dramatically now with high walls sheltering the milky-blue lake, the next destination, while Colle della Porta is ahead (E).

The tight zigzags that lead downwards have collapsed in parts but these can be easily bypassed and **Lago Lillet (2765m, 20min)** in its glacial cirque is soon reached. Surprisingly, the high-altitude desolate setting features the hardy orange and purple alpine toadflax and the tiny white blooms of chamois cress. See below for the exit to Mua from here.

Past the lakeside the path reappears and climbs gradually E with restful curves. Minor peaks La Cuccagna and Cima di Courmaon (SE) separate the path from the main valley now. N.550 follows an old moraine ridge and keeps right, avoiding the bulk of a permanent snow

*Rifugio Città di Chivasso*

The setting is an immense amphitheatre where walkers are mere dots against vast rubble slopes, traversed on wide zigzags.

*Approaching Colle della Porta*

field. A final curve left and you are at **Colle della Porta (3002m, 50min)**, the *porta* or door opening onto an ample wild basin in the shade of Testa del Gran Etrèt.

Head down the snow-covered slope, without losing sight of the vestiges of the track as it winds down the immense rubble-filled valley. You are led into the upper **Vallon del Roc**, below an imposing semicircle of peaks. Bivacco Giraudo, a small red hut, can be seen ENE. At about 2700m as a series of streams is crossed, the path heads decidedly down right in zigzags.

### Detour to Bivacco Giraudo (1h)

At this point, as long as visibility is good, those intending to break the walk and stay overnight at the bivouac hut should turn left at two small cairns. It is a matter of making your own way over fallen rocks, as no path as such exists for this stretch. Another stream needs to be crossed, then more clambering and past Lago Piatta to reach **Bivacco Ettore e Margherita Giraudo (2630m, 30min)**, only visible at the last moment. In mist or low cloud it could be tricky locating the hut. Meltwater is available nearby.

The descent is a little more straightforward, down an old game track SSE into the marshy basin (see

## WALK 20 – THE ROYAL TRACK TO CERESOLE REALE

below) past Alpe di Bruil (Alpe di Broglio) (2387m) to where cairns and the main track resume (30min).

From the Bivacco Giraudo turn-off, the main route descends for some way to reach a fertile marshy platform high above and overlooking a cluster of stone huts (Alpe Breuillet (Alpe Broglietto)). The path disappears for a while and only the occasional cairn or red stripe is to be found. Follow the lower edge of the shelf and prepare to ford the icy torrent, with the guarantee of a clearer path on the other side. Cairns reappear immediately as the route from Bivacco Giraudo joins up, and soon down right the wide track resumes its way, leading to a **2273m junction (1h40)** above a ruined group of stone huts, **Alpe Foges**.

Take the right branch (n.542 now) to a nearby spread of *roches moutonnées*. These aligned glacially-modelled boulders close off the mouth of a pretty marshy basin soft with cotton grass that houses the old Alpe Breuillet huts at the far end. Numerous ibex and chamois occupy these pastures, with the addition of the odd herd of cows. The path heads S now. Red paint marks the wide track, mostly on a level. Alpe Loserai di Sotto (2210m) is passed, a sizeable settlement comprising a variety of picturesque stone houses featuring intricate construction techniques. The track climbs a little in wide curves to **Colle Sia (2274m, 1h)**.

The descent starts in earnest and drops S down a bare hillside to more old stone buildings. At the 2000m mark you join the GTA (long-distance Grande Traversata delle Alpi) route! See below for the link with Vallon del Roc and Noasca. You soon reach scenically sited **Ca' Bianca (1942m)** in a clearing. From here the path heads decisively SW into a tall conifer wood, where woodpeckers and chamois are not uncommon. ▶ Laden raspberry thickets and laburnum announce the proximity of a dirt road and a park signpost. The main road is close by, as is a bus stop at Prese. The centre of **Ceresole Reale (1612m)** with shops,

Glimpses of the Ceresole Reale dam wall are frequent, but it never seems to get any closer.

tourist office and park visitor centre, is a 2km stroll right along the lakeside (1h40).

The village probably owes its name to 'cherries', whereas 'reale' (royal) was added in 1862 by King Vittorio Emanuele II, in exchange for concession of hunting rights for chamois and ibex. It is a peaceful place, with no tales of devils or evil doings, only fairies who leave gifts hanging in trees.

### Variation: Exit to Mua (2h)

Shortly after crossing the outlet from Lago Lillet, a cairn and red/white waymarking (right) indicate the long and steep but useful exit path for Mua. It drops S through a series of abandoned pasture and huts followed by larch forest, to emerge on the Col del Nivolet road at **Mua**, not far from **Rifugio Mila**, a campsite and the northernmost extremity of the Ceresole Reale lake.

### Variation: Link to Vallon del Roc (45min)

At the junction with the GTA after Colle Sia, it is feasible to branch off left (E) on the GTA to drop into Vallon del Roc and visit a string of fascinating abandoned hamlets, concluding at Noasca (see Walk 23).

---

**Col del Nivolet:** Rifugio Città di Chivasso tel 0124 953150 http://rifugiochivasso.altervista.org, CAI, sleeps 44, open late June to late Sept; Rifugio Savoia tel 0165 94141 www.rifugiosavoia.com, sleeps 60, open 15 June to 30 Sept; Rifugio Muzio tel 0124 953141 www.rifugiomuzio.net, CAI, sleeps 35, open May to Sept and weekends Mar, Apr and Oct; Bivacco Giraudo, CAI, sleeps 6, always open
**Ceresole Reale:** Albergo Sport tel 0124 953187 www.albergosportceresole.it; Chalet del Lago tel 0124 953128 www.chalet-ceresolereale.it
**Prese:** Posto Tappa GTA Fonti Minerali tel 347 7110309 www.fontiminerali.com, sleeps 20, open May to Sept

# WALK 21
*Sentiero Glaciologico Lago Serrù*

| | |
|---|---|
| **Time** | 2h |
| **Distance** | 5.8km/3.6 miles |
| **Ascent/descent** | 200m/200m |
| **Grade** | 1 |
| **Start/finish** | Car park below Lago Serrù dam |
| **Map** | L'Escursionista sheet 14, 1:25,000 |
| **Access** | Midsummer Sunday shuttle bus or car from Ceresole Reale, in turn served by year-round bus from the railhead of Pont Canavese. |

A fascinating and straightforward circular route conceived by experts and ice buffs to encourage people to admire and learn more about glacier-related phenomena. Ice used to lie at a depth of 200 metres in this basin, exerting amazing pressure on anything below. As the weighty frozen mass moved at a snail's pace downhill, it dragged over underlying rocks, smoothing their surface, although small stones and debris trapped beneath were caught up in the movement, leaving recognisable grooves and scratches. The glaciers in this southernmost valley have retreated a good 100 metres over the last 50 years, and are currently losing a metre a year in thickness. The glacial landscape is constantly altering.

This *sentiero glaciologico* (glacier path) steers well clear of crevasses and the like, following the banks of Lago Serrù, a natural lake enlarged for hydro-electric purposes in the late 1940s. Its water is cloudy with suspended rock dust and debris from the glaciers, causing the characteristic milky look, in sharp contrast to neighbouring Lago Agnel, crystal clear. At the walk start, the modest 'Glaciomuseo' museum about climate and glaciers (open 10am–4pm, mid-June to mid-Oct, free entry) occupies a former electricity board cabin. Natural science apart, it is a lovely walk in an inspiring setting. Late June to late September is the most suitable period to ensure that the path is snow-free. Note: On summer afternoons, the streams at the western end of the lake may be swollen with ice and snow melt so don't be surprised if you get your feet wet.

*Alpine asters*

For map see Walk 20

From the car park below the dam at **Lago Serrù (2275m)** walk uphill to the tower-like stone building housing the **Glaciomuseo**. Now ignore the markings for Colle della Losa and Pian della Ballotta and instead follow the red/white 'SG' markings SW along the lake's northern edge. This is an excellent angle for appreciating the Ghiacciaio della Capra (S). Covered with a thick carpet of rock debris, it spreads down the lower flanks of Cima d'Oin. Around the western end of the lake you cross the impetuous torrent of ice-melt from Pian Ballotta and a higher remnant glacier that transports glacial dust and debris, clouding the lake water. Further around another meltwater stream is crossed, and Lago Pratorotondo reached. Here turn right uphill for the recommended half-hour climb along the moraine crest to the edge of the **Ghiacciaio della Capra**.

Back down at water level, go right to the glacially-smoothed roches moutonées at the far end near the dam. It is only a short distance back to the **car park** or the bus stop from here.

---

**Col del Nivolet:** Rifugio Città di Chivasso tel 0124 953150 http://rifugiochivasso.altervista.org, CAI, sleeps 44, open late June to late Sept; Rifugio Savoia tel 0165 94141 www.rifugiosavoia.com, sleeps 60, open 15 June to 30 Sept
**Ceresole Reale:** Albergo Sport tel 0124 953187 www.albergosportceresole.it; Chalet del Lago tel 0124 953128 www.chalet-ceresolereale.it

## WALK 22
### Beneath the Tre Levanne

| | |
|---|---|
| Time | 6h30 |
| Distance | 14.7km/9.1 miles |
| Ascent/descent | 1050m/1050m |
| Grade | 2 |
| Start/finish | Ceresole Reale |
| Map | L'Escursionista sheet 14, 1:25,000 |
| Access | Ceresole Reale is served by year-round bus from the railhead of Pont Canavese. |

This rewarding itinerary in upper Valle dell'Orco is dominated by the three majestic Levanne peaks, as in fact is the entire valley between Col del Nivolet and the village of Ceresole Reale. The magnificent pyramidal line-up forms a stretch of the Italian–French border. The walk as far as convivial Rifugio Jervis is easy and the ample panoramic flats and immense glacially smoothed rock slabs in the vicinity of the refuge are perfect for relaxing picnics. The continuation over Col di Nel is less frequented, apart from the chamois and marmots, and, while steep in parts, is relatively trouble-free. Snow cover on this stretch may persist into July. The complete walk circuit returns to Ceresole Reale; however, those with a car may prefer to park at Villa and return there afterwards on the marginally shorter variant given.

Just up from the church on the main road at **Ceresole Reale (1612m)**, a path breaks off left with steps down for the 'Passeggiata Lago', lakeside promenade. At the water's edge turn right (NW) and continue to the far end. At Rifugio Mila, near the hydro-electric works, join the road past the campsite and cluster of cafés that go by the name of **Villa (1583m, 30min)**. Immediately after a small chapel is the start of path n.530 signposted for Rifugio Jervis.

A clear path with occasional red paint splashes, it crosses a stream then climbs W through a fresh larch wood alive with song birds. Alpe Foiera (1753m) is the

For map see Walk 20

first of a series of old abandoned summer farms passed, beside a stream which is repeatedly crisscrossed. A second group of huts, A. Bagnetti (1877m), occupies a picturesque marshy area dotted with fluffy cotton grass and bordered by rowan trees. Larch and pink alpenrose shrubs then accompany you to a marvellous lookout point where views take in Punta di Galisia and Punta Basei (WNW), as well as a glimpse of the Levanne themselves. At **Alpe Degrane (2049m)** you head S and out of the trees and the *rifugio* soon comes into sight. High left above cascading Rio di Nel in its narrow gorge, the path winds through shrubs and bears right over glacially smoothed rock and across a bridge.

**Rifugio Jervis (2250m, 2h)**, a well-run alpine hut with helpful staff, was named after Guglielmo Iervis, a World War I partisan and mountaineer from Ivrea, a town at the easternmost end of Valle d'Aosta and home to the CAI branch that owns the refuge. Its position is enthusing, before the three Levanne peaks which shelter the Ghiacciaio di Nel and its old moraine ridges. Furthermore it stands on the very edge of the panoramic Piano di Nel, an ample basin excavated by an extensive glacier and successively occupied by a lake, now silted up. The small pumping station is connected to the Villa hydro-electric power station.

*Rifugio Jervis*

## WALK 22 – BENEATH THE TRE LEVANNE

Back at the bridge walk past the pumps for faintly marked n.526, which skirts the easternmost edge of the basin. Head for the stone buildings of Alpe di Nel (2264m), keeping a watchful eye out for squelchy marshes. As you enter a final cirque, fork sharp left at a prominent cairn. Mostly E the path climbs steadily and steeply over brightly flowered mixed rock-earth terrain, with some snow cover to be expected early summer. Chamois are a common sight. **Col di Nel (2551m, 1h15)** occupies an excellent position for appreciating the magnificent head of the valley, taking in the Ceresole Reale lake. ▶ The clear descent path drops E quickly down grassy flowered slopes over a series of small platforms, plenty of helpful cairns showing the way. After a stretch alongside an old rockslip, you reach a boggy lake then the modest peak La Trucci. The path soon bears S dropping into a vast pasture basin. ▶ At what must have been a sizeable farming settlement (A. Pian Mutta, 2130m), pick your way through the ruins and across a shallow earth gully. Turn left along the grassy ridge to an old stone hut, referred to as **Trucco (2098m, 1h)** on most maps.

Ignore the fork right for Bivacco Leonesi and proceed E across marshy terrain, perfect for the tiny purplish-white flowers of insect-devourer common butterwort. A path turns uphill for Lago Dres, but you descend NE towards the lake. A broad lane on the water's edge is finally reached. Here turn right along to the dam wall which is traversed. Keep hugging the water's edge for a short stretch as you approach the park visitor centre, then fork right back up to **Ceresole Reale (1612m, 1h45)**.

Silver-bearing lead, commonly found in Valle dell'Orco, was once mined in the vicinity of the pass, by Christians as legend would have it.

The flowers are brighter and thicker now, notably gentians and yellow avens.

### Variant: Alternative return to Villa (1h20)

From Trucco, take the path that descends N for the most part, into tall conifer woods, punctuated by oversized red ant nests. It emerges at the houses of **Pouvens** (1598m) on the lakeside. Turn left along the narrow road past the power station and back to **Villa (1583m)**.

*Pasque flowers*

Rifugio Jervis tel 0124 953140 www.rifugiojervis.com, CAI, sleeps 26, open 1 July to 31Aug and weekends in June and Sept
**Villa:** Rifugio Mila tel 0124 953230 or 340 0556496, sleeps 25, open weekends and 15 June to 15 Sept www.rifugiomila.it
**Ceresole Reale:** Albergo Sport tel 0124 953187 www.albergosportceresole.it; Chalet del Lago tel 0124 953128 www.chalet-ceresolereale.it

# WALK 23
## The Villages of Valle Dell'Orco

| | |
|---|---|
| **Time** | 3h |
| **Distance** | 6.3km/3.9 miles |
| **Ascent/descent** | 470m/470m |
| **Grade** | 1–2 |
| **Start/finish** | Sentiero Natura marker at 1195m on the road uphill from Noasca |
| **Map** | L'Escursionista sheet 14, 1:25,000 |
| **Access** | Noasca is on the year-round bus line from the railhead of Pont Canavese. Some 1.5km above Noasca is the start of the 'Sentiero Natura'. Ask the driver to drop you off here, mentioning the old villages by name. Car owners can park on the main road where it widens after the hairpin bends above Noasca and prior to the road tunnel. |

In Valle dell'Orco, an intriguing round trip on an old paved path that threads its way through some unique alpine villages, dating back to at least the 1700s and only recently abandoned. The cause was mainly migration to the industrial cities for work. Wandering through the peaceful overgrown settlements disturbed only by the odd barking dog belonging to the reticent shepherds who make their summer residence here, modern-day visitors can get a feeling of what medium-altitude (1500m) mountain life used to be like. Strictly local materials, namely stone and some timber, were used to craft houses and huts built around huge fallen boulders, available space and 'free' walls exploited to the utmost.

Apart from communal buildings such as a church, school and oven for the traditional rye bread, there are fascinating colourful religious frescoes and numerous family votive shrines along the way. A special mention is due the ingenious *crutin*, low stone-roofed huts used for dairy storage – villagers would divert watercourses through the huts to keep the products cool. While in the Valle dell'Orco make sure you purchase some delicious *toma*, the local cheese that used to be made in villages such as these.

*Gran Paradiso – Alta Via 2 Trek and Day Walks*

A whole day could be spent exploring the string of hamlets and wandering along the paths, which comprise the sole connection with the valley, apart from the rare later addition of one or two mechanised cable-ways. After a climb to the first village, the route is level, then a final descent past lower Vallon del Roc leads back to the main road near the start point. Any time between April and November is suitable for this easy route.

On the roadside at 1195m, look for the national park wooden post for the start of the 'Sentiero Natura' together with the distinctive red/white of the long-distance GTA (Grande Traversata delle Alpi). The path winds upwards through hazel trees to old terracing for cultivation, now inhabited by bright green lizards and butterflies. A narrow asphalt road is crossed and you traverse the hamlet of **Balmarossa di Sopra (1275m)**. After re-crossing the road, the old paved path soon appears and climbs high on the left bank of Torrente Ciamosseretto, the cause of noticeable damage downstream at Noasca. After a couple more encounters with the road you reach a small parking area (1400m). Ignore the detour right across the cascading torrent and keep straight on up the path, wider and in better condition now, to wind up through rich mixed woods including wild cherry, sycamore and chestnut. Dry-stone walls border long stretches of paved path and shrines have been fitted into niches.

The first settlement, **Varda (1500m)**, demands an exploratory detour off the main path. After a stream

## WALK 23 – THE VILLAGES OF VALLE DELL'ORCO

crossing further on around the hillside is **Maison** (Meison) **(1567m)**. This is the largest village and has some fascinating constructions, starting with the diminutive whitewashed church decorated with paintings of saints. On the far edge of the village is the school complete with old wooden benches, chilly outside toilet and teachers' lodgings upstairs. It was in use until the mid-1960s.

A brief climb leads to a marvellous panoramic stretch on a cliff edge with giddy views to the Valle dell'Orco road and underlying hamlets. Ahead W is the Cima di Courmaon. The next settlement, **Mola (1591m)**, with its communal oven and bright frescoes, is the highest of this line of hamlets, followed shortly by **Cappelle (1585m)** which features a drinking fountain and barking dogs. A brief descent through tall grass takes you to the torrent and the cluster of huts that comprise **Potes (1500m, 1h40)**, below a lovely waterfall.

Across the torrent after a bridge crossing, the path climbs onto a rocky spur below a chapel and the hamlet of **Borgo Vecchio (1567m)**. At this point the red/white GTA climbs away to the right whereas the Sentiero Natura starts its descent down the valley. Flowered pastures are crossed followed by a further brief climb. Once you have passed a side watercourse in light woodland, the path reappears in paved form intent on serious descent at last. Zigzags lead to the tightly-knit houses of **Fregai (1428m)**. Soon you drop unexpectedly into a delicious beech wood, which lasts the rest of the way down to the settlement of **Pianchette (1220m)**. Thread your way through the old and new houses, complete with frescoes and inhabitants, down to the road. Turn left here and proceed to where the main road from Ceresole Reale emerges from the tunnel, in the vicinity of a bus stop. The start point is a short stroll downhill (1h20).

**Noasca:** Hotel La Cascata tel 340 4729334 www.lacascatahotel.it

## WALK 24
### Beyond the Dam in Vallone di Piantonetto

| | |
|---|---|
| Time | 2h15 |
| Distance | 5.3km/3.2 miles |
| Ascent/descent | 410m/410m |
| Grade | 1–2 |
| Start/finish | Lago di Teleccio dam |
| Map | L'Escursionista sheet 15, 1:25,000 |
| Access | From Rosone in Valle dell'Orco, drive past the hamlet of San Lorenzo (hotel-restaurant) all the way up Vallone di Piantonetto and park near the guardian's house at the top of the dam wall. The road is narrow but was improved and surfaced in 2006. |

The inclusion of an itinerary in a valley whose upper reaches have been dammed for hydro-electricity purposes may seem incongruous. However, with its towering gneiss flanks, long desolate Vallone di Piantonetto is a curious anomaly. Above the dam a beautiful ample grazing basin is revealed, surrounded by a series of vast rock shelves, precursors to a chain of imposing peaks, the likes of Roccia Viva and Torre del Gran San Pietro. Sheltering in cirques are two surviving glacier pockets, which feed both the pastures and the dam.

A refuge stands on the edge of the basin, a testimony to the growing popularity of this wild and wonderful valley with walkers and rock climbers. The walk described here is a straightforward and very rewarding circuit with wonderful views. As the initial stretch as far as Rifugio Pontese is only faintly marked, it is inadvisable in low cloud or mist, whereas the return is wide and clear. A couple of days could profitably be spent at the friendly hut with side trips to neighbouring passes and valleys.

Construction of the 23 million cubic metre dam, on the site of a pre-existing silted-up glacial lake, dates back to 1955. In combination with flows from the similarly dammed lakes of Ceresole Reale, Valsoera and Eugio, it supplies the historic power plant at Rosone. A 2km-long underground passage

## WALK 24 – BEYOND THE DAM IN VALLONE DI PIANTONETTO

carries a gigantic conduit – and staff members – beneath the mountains on the east side to connect with the dam of Lago di Valsoera. The extensive hydro-electric system in this southern sector of the park is supervised by the Torino(Turin)-based electricity board AEM (Azienda Energetica Municipale) which started operations in the Valle dell'Orco back in the 1920s.

Start out from the car park at the wall of the **Lago di Teleccio dam (1917m)**. Rifugio Pontese is visible N in a commanding position, a dark building with yellow shutters. However, well beyond it tower Torre del Gran San Pietro (NNW), with massive Becco di Valsoera (N). Turn left and walk all the way along the 80m high, 515m-long wall and then go right (NW) to join a faint path marked with yellow paint splashes that heads across to the buildings of summer farm **Alpe Fumietto (2182m)**. Ignore the path (n.555) that forks left and continue N past long-abandoned Alpe Mandonera (2265m) and Alpe Giafort (2236m). Here you bear E to join the path from Colle dei Becchi, and soon drop to the vast glacially smoothed rock slab where homely **Rifugio Pontese (2200m, 1h30)** stands. An earlier hut built in 1889 at the time when the surrounding peaks were being discovered by the pioneer alpinists, stood much further up the valley. The amphitheatre, clockwise from W, encompasses Blanc Giuir, Becco della Tribolazione, Becca di Gay, Roccia Viva, Torre del Gran San Pietro, Punta d'Ondezana and Becco di Valsoera, which average out at 3500m.

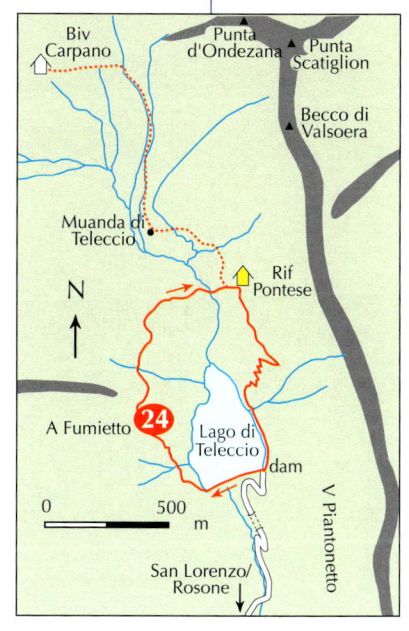

### Side trip to Muanda di Teleccio (30min return)

Mandatory path n.558 proceeds NW keeping to the right bank of the main torrent. It quickly reaches a glacial cirque and vast pasture basin watered by streams fed from the higher glaciers – Ghiacciaio di Teleccio (due N behind a rock barrier) and Ghiacciaio Roccia Viva (NW).

The marshy terrain hosts specialised flowers such as the insectivorous common butterwort with its small purplish-white blooms, and the solitary whitish flowers of grass-of-Parnassus.

Not far along are the old huts known as **Muanda di Teleccio (2217m)**, the term denoting a high-altitude summer farm. Reference to a nearby property has surfaced from medieval records as the inhabitants of Cogne were granted pasture rights there in 1206 by the Bishop of Aosta. Payment took the form of 30 cheeses to be delivered on St Martin's Day, 11 November. To reach the site from the N, however, the shepherds were obliged to undertake the lengthy traverse of Colle di Teleccio (3304m).

Today, in place of the livestock are large numbers of chamois – shy creatures who make for the surrounding slopes if disturbed. Marmots are not unusual either. (Visible on a further rock shelf NW is **Bivacco Carpano**. At 2865m it is a destination for experienced walkers only as the faintly marked path has both steep and exposed stretches, aided in parts. Allow 3h return time.) Return to Rifugio Pontese the same way.

From Rifugio Pontese a clear path heads SSE in descent over a rock spur and winds down a rock flank (ignore the junction for difficult path n.560 to Rifugio Pocchiola-Meneghello). It widens into a broad track and follows the E shore of the lake to the jumble of derelict buildings and the **Lago di Teleccio dam** wall **(1917m, 45min)**.

*WALK 25 – NIVOLASTRO TO ANDORINA*

Rifugio Pontese tel 0124 800186 www.rifugiopontese.it; Club Alpinistico Pontese, sleeps 70, open mid-June to mid-Sept and weekends 1 to 15 June, 15 Sept to 15 Oct; Bivacco Carpano, sleeps 7, always open, has blankets and cooking gear. Water can be found 150 metres away – follow the cairns.

## WALK 25
*Nivolastro to Andorina*

| | |
|---|---|
| Time | 3h30 |
| Distance | 9.7km/6 miles |
| Ascent/descent | 670m/670m |
| Grade | 2 |
| Start/finish | Ronco Canavese |
| Map | L'Escursionista sheet 15, 1:25,000 |
| Access | Ronco Canavese and Valprato are served by a year-round bus service from the railhead at Pont Canavese. |

This beautiful and not-too-strenuous circuit explores two abandoned alpine hamlets set in marvellously scenic spots and rarely visited. It runs along the eastern flanks of Valle Soana, the name possibly derived from *suina*, pork-related, or alternatively *sana*, healthy, which the locals prefer. Thickly wooded, it is becoming popular with destructive but shy wild boar, now hunted by the rangers. Note: this route has only recently been waymarked and may not be shown on all maps.

From **Ronco Canavese (940m)** opposite Albergo Centrale take narrow Via Vittorio Emanuele uphill past the bakery to the old people's home (Istituto San Giuseppe) where you take a concrete ramp left, signed for Nivolastro. After a stream crossing it becomes a delightful paved and stepped mule track climbing the steep mountain flank

## GRAN PARADISO – ALTA VIA 2 TREK AND DAY WALKS

quite effortlessly in easy curves. Panoramic outcrop Mont del Trasi is followed by the first of a curious series of arched shrines dedicated to San Grato (see Walk 18), the Madonna and others. The surroundings are beautiful woodland, both conifer and deciduous, inhabited by noisy nutcrackers. A curious monolithic stone watering trough precedes your arrival at the well-kept church of San Grato and drinking fountain at **Nivolastro (1423m, 1h15)**.

Ignore the signed path to Chiapetto and make your way past erstwhile elegant multi-storied houses with their iron balconies. With the exception of the ranger's premises, the hamlet is slowly and surely crumbling and giving in to ferocious creepers. On the far edge of the settlement take the narrow marked path N along old stone terracing walls and into woods, home to chamois. Larch and alpenrose grow side by side with huge ant hills. You find yourself climbing gently to the 1500m mark in order to avoid sheer rock outcrops. Cascading streams over glacially smoothed rock slabs are crossed on a bridge, then not far along is the scenically-set stone chapel and silent old houses of **Andorina (1453m, 1h)**.

After drinking in the wonderful views which take in the Rosa dei Banchi (N), set out on the path marked 'V' (for Valprato). It is a straightforward descent NE initially through pine woods then beautiful tall beech. You emerge on the roadside close to Chiesale and turn right for the short walk down to **Valprato Soana (1116m, 45min)** with its eateries and tourist office. Now either take the bus to return to **Ronco Canavese** or follow the road on foot (allow 30min).

## WALK 25 – NIVOLASTRO TO ANDORINA

*The bridge en route to Andorina*

## WALK 26
*Frescoes and Fridges en route to Bivacco Davito*

| | |
|---|---|
| **Time** | 6h |
| **Distance** | 12.4km/7.7 miles |
| **Ascent/descent** | 1175m/1175m |
| **Grade** | 2 |
| **Start/finish** | Tressi |
| **Map** | L'Escursionista sheet 15, 1:25,000 |
| **Access** | The start is accessible by car. By public transport, the Val di Forzo turn-off (at Bosco, 1km before Ronco Canavese) is the closest bus stop on the year-round Pont Canavese–Valprato Soana line. The 5km walk up the asphalt road to Tressi is not unpleasant and the locals are not adverse to hitchhikers but traffic is light. |

Added to the national park in 1979, quiet Val di Forzo branches off Valle Soana to run in a northwesterly direction. Its northernmost fork culminates in a vast wild rock-strewn cirque in the shade of little-known giants Monveso di Forzo, Punta di Forzo and elegant Torre di Lavina. While the walk has Bivacco Davito and its desolate setting as its destination, the fascinating first stage uses an old paved access path to the now abandoned hamlet of Boschiettiera, well worth a visit for a glimpse of the past world of medium-altitude alpine life. En route are rock niches housing colourful frescoed votive shrines dating back to the 1700s, possibly the work of itinerant artists as a certain similarity in style can be observed in the historic religious frescoes throughout these southern valleys.

While the walk is rather lengthy, there is plenty of variety and the good condition of the path makes it suitable for all abilities. As far as Bivacco Davito goes, the tiny basic metallic hut stands in a particularly isolated position, making an overnight stay there a special experience. A sleeping bag and cooking gear are needed, while water can be taken from the nearby stream. No accommodation is available in the valley, making Ronco Canavese the closest useful base with its shops and hotel.

*WALK 26 – FRESCOES AND FRIDGES EN ROUTE TO BIVACCO DAVITO*

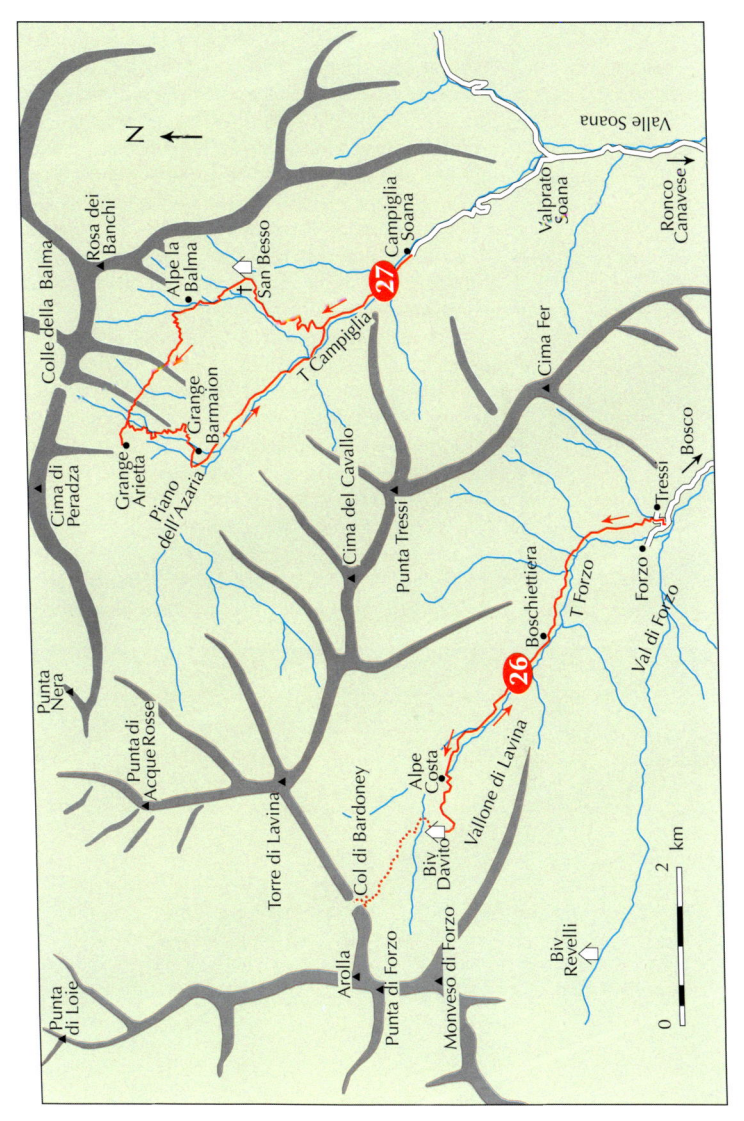

## Gran Paradiso – Alta Via 2 Trek and Day Walks

*Note: in low cloud or mist, common in these high valleys, orientation can be tricky above the tree line.*

On the final curves of the road, marked path n.608 forks off left, just before you reach **Tressi (1185m)**. It bypasses the hamlet, and, bearing left (N), crosses a dry torrent bed. The old path (frequent red waymarking) proceeds between low stone walls through abandoned orchards and meadows. An easy climb through hazel trees brings you onto a rocky rise on the right bank of impetuous Torrente Forzo opposite old stone houses. Steps cut out of the rock lead to an exceptional example of religious folk art, a wayside votive shrine under an impressive rock overhang. Dating back to 1748, it is often lovingly restored, hence the gorgeous colours of its multitudinous saints.

A side stream is crossed and the path continues climbing as the valley narrows. Next to a rustic bridge n.610 turns up right through swathes of yellow broom to the hamlet of Boschietto, visible on a rise with its white church tower (a worthwhile detour, time permitting). N.608 continues W alongside the ice-blue torrent and traverses meadows with ash and sycamore trees to the once-thriving settlement of **Boschiettiera (1486m, 1h10)**. Nowadays it has only a few summertime

*Frescoed shrine en route to Boschiettiera*

## Walk 26 – Frescoes and Fridges en route to Bivacco Davito

residents, drinking water and a communal oven, not to mention more intriguing votive frescoes.

This upper section of Val di Forzo is called Vallone di Lavina. Keep on up the right side of the torrent, NW now. Steeper stretches pass through larch wood with plenty of wild berries. As the gradient levels somewhat among the last larch trees, the valley opens out with a lovely vision of a broad rock platform, legacy of an ancient glacier, beyond which is a light grey semicircular ridge. Torre di Lavina is N, and, despite its name, is more like a pyramid than a tower. After crossing a small stream on boulders, you then come to several abandoned huts on a rise (Grangia Pian Lavina, 1796m), with a second group huddling beneath a rock overhang a little further up. Consider yourself halfway at this point. The path bears left across another dry watercourse and steps cut into the rock climb in a zigzag through spreads of alpenrose and green alder shrubs. A pasture clearing is studded with an amazing concentration of black vanilla orchids, while a signboard reminds you these are the preserver of the national park.

Yet another stream is crossed beneath a small waterfall, and you wind up to more old stone huts, **Alpe Costa (1979m)**, where a rest will give you time to admire views SE down the valley. The grazing cows in the vicinity are brought up for the summer pastures but the shepherd is rarely in residence, preferring the comfort of his village. The landscape becomes more desolate with every step you take and the path is not always clear, although there are enough cairns and red paint splashes to guide you. There is a further group of huts (Grangia Lavinetta, 2092m) in a lovely basin run through with rivulets which make for marshy terrain and wet feet. Several curious huts here are low, turf-roofed affairs called *crutin*, which, rather than providing dwellings for alpine dwarves, once served as cool storage of dairy products – primitive precursors of the refrigerator.

Continue up past a collapsed hut, directly above which a sizeable cairn is visible (on the edge of the platform where the bivouac hut is located). The path, clearer now, heads left below it, with a final wide swing right to come out onto the rock platform where you eventually reach the yellow-painted **Bivacco Davito (2360m, 2h30)**.

### Extension: to Col di Bardoney (2h30 return)
Experienced walkers (only) can proceed NW for the remaining 500m in ascent to **Col di Bardoney (2833m)** (allow 1h30). The pass had a bad reputation in the past for the unusual number of fatal accidents that overtook the Val Soana coppersmiths travelling north in search of work, despite a well-used mule track which has now totally disappeared. From the pass it is possible to descend into Vallon de Bardoney (see Walk 2) and continue to Lillaz and Cogne. This would make a very long itinerary and there is no accommodation before Lillaz.

From Bivacco Davito, return to **Tressi** the same way, allowing 2h20.

### Alternative: towards Bivacco Revelli
The other major arm of Val di Forzo separates off at the village of Forzo to run westward (on path n.604). While not described in detail here it is also good walking territory. Another unmanned hut, Bivacco Revelli, is to be found in its upper reaches at 2610m, 4h by signed path (n.605) from Forzo.

---

Bivacco Davito, CAI, sleeps 4, always open; Bivacco Revelli, CAI, sleeps 6, always open

## WALK 27
### Sanctuary of San Besso

| | |
|---|---|
| Time | 5h30 |
| Distance | 13.3km/8.2 miles |
| Ascent/descent | 1050m/1050m |
| Grade | 2 |
| Start/finish | Campiglia Soana |
| Map | L'Escursionista sheet 15, 1:25,000 |
| Access | Campiglia can be reached on the summer bus extension (mid-June to mid-September) from Valprato Soana, 2.5km downhill, where the service terminates at other times. The line originates at the Pont Canavese railhead. |

An engrossing combination of ancient legend and Christian beliefs, centred on an early martyr and possibly the area's first evangelist, Besso, comes into play here. A Roman soldier in the Thebean legion, in all likelihood dark-skinned, Besso escaped persecution in Martigny in the 3rd century AD and took refuge in the upper reaches of Valle Soana. However, after a period spent successfully converting the local shepherds, he was hunted out and unceremoniously thrown off a high rock overhang. Not long afterwards, on 1 December (which then became the saint's day) shepherds recovered the body by digging where blood stains appeared on the snow.

Today a sanctuary in his name stands beneath that outcrop, Monte Fauterio in Val Campiglia. Festivities are also held on 10 August, attended by the faithful and hangers-on in long processions. Year in year out a group of pilgrims from Cogne unfailingly cross the mountains to participate, consolidating age-old links and traditions. After the celebratory mass, the weighty statue of the saint, dressed as a Roman centurion, is carried around the sanctuary by bearers who vie with each other for the honour (perhaps by offering the largest sum of money). At the head is the scarlet-robed priest bearing the revered relics of the saint. In addition, a curious habit is associated with the sanctuary of giving away fragments of greenstone as a lucky charm, as it is believed to have miraculous properties. Scholars have linked this to both

*Gran Paradiso – Alta Via 2 Trek and Day Walks*

ancient pagan cult practices as well as San Besso himself, well known for his powers of healing.

Apart from the rewarding loop walk described here, which includes a beautiful panoramic traverse with only the occasional crumbly exposed stretch, the ascent as far as the sanctuary is a worthwhile excursion in its own right. Marmots and a wealth of wild flowers are guaranteed, while those who venture higher up will be rewarded by the sight of chamois. As relatively low altitudes are involved, the walk is usually feasible as early as June and as late as October, although this will depend on snow falls.

Campiglia has no shops, so buy picnic supplies at Valprato. Walkers can stay overnight at the recently renovated *ricovero*, a self-catering refuge with decent facilities. You need to phone beforehand for the key: tel 333 7241229 or 335 7499274.

For map see Walk 26

From the bus stop near the World War I cenotaph at **Campiglia Soana (1350m)**, follow the road uphill NW past the former hotel and car park. The way is soon unsurfaced and closed to unauthorised traffic, and you cross a wooden bridge to the right side of Torrente Campiglia. As the watercourse cascades away, you continue steadily upwards to the clear turn-off right, marked for San Besso. Path n.625 climbs N through light mixed woods with elder and raspberry shrubs, while the open mountainside is thick with the blooms of the martagon lily and purple orchids which attract fluttering colourful butterflies. A diagonal passage left climbs past a rock outcrop and up to an old hut (at about 1800m), with a good view NW to the upper valley.

The path veers left (N) to enter a side valley with simple summer farm, Grangia Ciavanis (1876m), and its cloud of flies, not far from a lovely waterfall. The sanctuary buildings are visible now NE, in the shelter of the pointed rock overhang Monte Fauterio, on the lower reaches of Rosa dei Banchi. The way up the steep flank twists and turns, slippery underfoot at times due to the presence of greenstone, which is abundant here. The rock, basic in geological terms, also means that the terrain is suitable for purple alpine asters, pink thrift and

## WALK 27 – SANCTUARY OF SAN BESSO

felted edelweiss, which brighten the meadows above the sanctuary, perfect for picnics. Adjoining the **Santuario di San Besso (2019m, 2h)** is the Ricovero Bausano bivouac hut. The church itself is locked but the statue of San Besso, as a Roman centurion, can be made out inside.

Signposted path n.625 skirts beneath the church and bivouac building to head NW across pasture dotted with wild flowers. Several side streams are crossed, but keep to the right side of the main watercourse, Rio San Besso, for the time being. However, from the cluster of huts, **Alpe la Balma (2152m)**, go sharp left down across the probably dry stream bed. A dirt path soon becomes evident climbing a ridge W towards a depression. These southernmost flanks are carpeted with alpenrose, and chamois are often visible. From a first saddle aim for the low depression straight ahead. (Don't be tempted by the cairns that lead up right – the route for Colle della Balma.)

From the next saddle (2400m, 1h), Val di Campiglia opens up dizzily at your feet, and there are views W towards its head and Torre di Lavina (WSW).

The narrow but clear path now bears right (WNW).

*Santuario di San Besso under Monte Fauterio*

*The unstable nature of the terrain is due to the succession of different geological strata.*

The traverse consists essentially of alternating ups and downs, with several stretches where the rubble-earth mixture has given way. It is a little slippery when wet, necessitating extra care. ◄ After contouring along the S flank of Rosa dei Banchi, the shepherds' huts of **Grange Arietta (2288m, 45min)** in their pasture basin are reached.

(A path continues NW to 2939m Col d'Arietta, the connecting pass for Cogne and the age-old route used by its inhabitants. The original path has reportedly all but disappeared in the immediate vicinity of the pass, and the crossing is for experienced walkers.)

Go back briefly along the path you arrived on, then turn down right on n.624. It drops to cross a stream near a waterfall. Larch trees start gradually and the path winds down SSW, steeply at times, in their meagre shade. As the valley floor is approached, keep to the left of the farm buildings of **Grange Barmaion (1651m)** to reach the vehicle access track. Once one of the king's game routes, it runs SE along the delightful **Piano dell'Azaria**. This quiet, ample valley has several modest dairy farms. The return walk is a pleasant stroll on the left bank of the wide torrent. After the San Besso turn-off is passed, it is over the bridge and down to **Campiglia Soana (1h45)** where the walk started.

## WALK 28
*Col Larissa*

| | |
|---|---|
| Time | 5h |
| Distance | 10.8km/6.7 miles |
| Ascent/descent | 1030m/1030m |
| Grade | 2 |
| Start/finish | Piamprato |
| Map | L'Escursionista sheet 15, 1:25,000 |
| Access | A midsummer bus from Pont Canavese ventures up the ever-narrowing 5.7km road to the start point at Piamprato. At other times it terminates at Valprato Soana. The walk extension concludes at Chardonney, which has year-round buses to the railway station at Hône-Bard in Valle d'Aosta. (See Stage 1 of Alta Via 2.) |

An interesting walk in itself, especially for the wide-ranging outlook from Col Larissa, this route could be useful for trekking from the southern Valle Soana to the Valle di Champorcher and Valle d'Aosta – not to mention joining the AV2. It was long used by the locals for this purpose, not to mention the king's hunting parties on the 19th-century game track constructed through the pass. Long, paved stretches have survived and help render it trouble-free for today's walkers. Wild flower enthusiasts will be delighted by the vast range encountered, especially on the final approach to the pass, which makes midsummer the best time to go.

Nowadays hardly anyone stays on through winter at the village of Piamprato – recent reports put the number at five. The large church and numerous old stone buildings dating back to the 1700s are indicators of a former permanent sizeable community. Before that, chronicles from the 1600s recount a devastating avalanche that completely swept the village away.

From the parking area and bus stop at **Piamprato (1551m)**, head N straight through the village, with an eye out for the old school on the left. A 19th-century plaque on its wall expresses gratitude to the king, their benefactor.

## Gran Paradiso – Alta Via 2 Trek and Day Walks

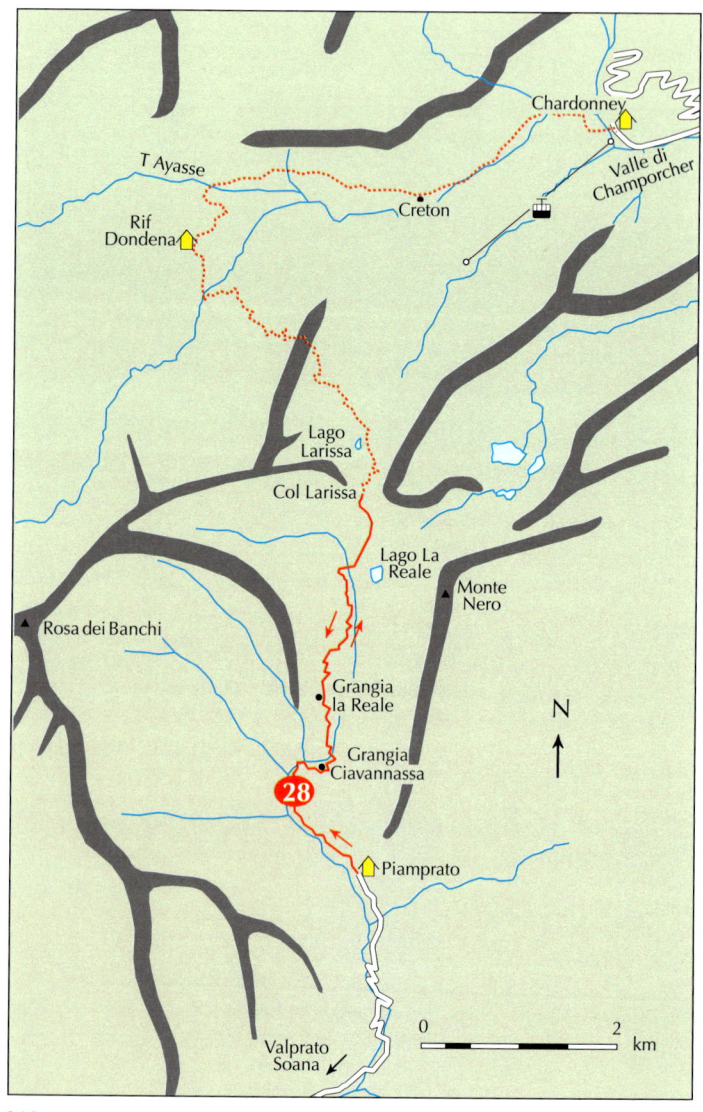

## WALK 28 – COL LARISSA

Take the dirt road (n.630) N alongside the torrent. Pass old farm buildings and several wide bends before the road ends. Repeated flood damage has washed away sections of the original path so follow the newer path up right. You make your way up dark grassy banks (red/white waymarking reappears from time to time) to the low farm buildings belonging to **Grangia Ciavannassa (1865m)**. Latecomers might glimpse the bats from the retinue of a past resident, a terrible witch. Climb up behind the first building to the higher constructions. From here the regularly marked path keeps left above the watercourse, ascending due N in zigzags.

The route emerges onto a lovely flat basin brightened by pink alpenrose shrubs and heads briefly left (W) across the torrent and up to an old-style summer sheep farm, **Grangia La Reale (2095m)**. The King of Sardinia apparently had a lead mine in the vicinity which explains the denomination 'reale', royal. However, in-depth studies have suggested that the name dates back to the 1700s and probably derives from an ancient Piemontese word for 'stream'.

You soon enter the domain of the national park, and, as though to confirm the fact that the area is under special protection, masses of pink hairy primroses carpet the slopes. The path climbs easily through a series of upper valleys and the pass soon comes into view, easily identifiable thanks to a pylon.

The mountain NE, Monte Nero, was another scene of evildoing. A devil once tricked the villagers of Piamprato into gathering below it to await the Madonna, who in fact appeared just in time to stop the rocks crashing onto the onlookers, as per the dreadful original plan!

At about 2400m the path turns right to cross the torrent. Cairns point up to where vestiges of the royal game track are obvious above picturesque Lago La Reale (2412m). It leads across grass studded with lilac round-leaved penny-cress, then rubble, with white glacier crowfoot blooms. A long diagonal stretch completes the ascent to **Col Larissa (2584m, 3h)**, the name derived from 'larch'. In clear conditions the spectacular views

# GRAN PARADISO – ALTA VIA 2 TREK AND DAY WALKS

*On the way to Col Larissa*

from this ample saddle range from the triangle of Rosa dei Banchi and its small glacier (WSW), then the first line of mountains to the N, including Monte Avic towering over its lake, further behind which, with any luck, the Matterhorn and Monte Rosa will be visible. Views S even take in Monviso and the Maritime Alps.

Unless you decide to extend the walk (below), return to **Piamprato** the same way, allowing 2h.

### Extension via Rifugio Dondena to Chardonney (3h15)

You are not likely to meet many other walkers on this lovely stretch. From **Col Larissa (2584m)** over predominantly greenstone, follow the clear path N downhill. Snow usually lies late here but the old wide game track is soon clear. You pass **Lago Larissa (2486m)**, but the most striking feature of this area is the vivacity of the spreads of flowers. You will be dazzled by the tiny blue jewelled clumps of gentians, large bright violets, a variety of saxifrages, as well as the insignificant-looking but aromatic yellow genepi, used for flavouring a local spirit. After crossing a small watercourse (at about 2400m), the track climbs to the top of a ski lift (2480m). Edelweiss and thrift flower on the calcareous terrain here. Views include Mont Glacier (NW) and even far-off Monte Rosa (NE). The track winds down W into the Vallone dei Banchi, the stream of meltwater from the glacier beneath Rosa dei Banchi (SW now). At an old stone hut (2300m) there is a shortcut down to the bridge and over to **Rifugio Dondena (2200m, 1h15)**. The hospitality and cuisine (such as roast meats accompanied by polenta and local mushrooms) make up for the rather bare concrete building, which is surprisingly a converted royal hunting lodge. Walkers intending to embark on the long-distance Alta Via 2 can do so here. (See Stage 2 of the AV2.)

Leave the building down the wide dirt road that leads E past old barracks and through pasture to a parking area and soon the fork right where black/yellow AV2 waymarking points down right along the original royal game track. After the hamlet of **Creton (1873m)** your route heads S, winding down to the Torrente Ayasse and across two wooden bridges then past a ski lift. The path immerses itself in a shady mixed wood, including masses of wild roses and alpenrose beneath larch and green alder. The stream in the meantime is crashing its way through a narrow neck.

Red-eyed Apollo butterflies abound in a clearing with old huts and a cross, then it is back into the final stretch of wood, with delicate laburnum blossoms. Tight curves lead below the Laris cable car until you arrive finally at **Chardonney (1448m, 2h)**. (See AV2 start for facilities.)

## Gran Paradiso – Alta Via 2 Trek and Day Walks

**Piamprato:** Agriturismo Aquila Bianca tel 0124 812993 sleeps 20, open May to Oct http://locandaaquilabianca.wixsite.com/piamprato; Rifugio Dondena tel (mobile) 348 2664837, sleeps 80, open mid-June to mid-Sept www.rifugidelarosa.it.
**Chardonney:** Hotel Chardoney tel 0125 376011 www.hotelchardoney.com. Grocery shops.

*Lago La Reale and Monte Nero*

# APPENDIX A
## Italian–English Glossary

| | |
|---|---|
| *acqua (non) potabile* | water (not) suitable for drinking |
| *affittacamere* | B&B |
| *agibile (inagibile)* | in good (bad) condition, referring to a hut or route |
| *aiuto!* | help! |
| *albergo* | hotel |
| *alpage, alpe* | summer pasture area and/or hut |
| *alta via* | long distance high level route |
| *alto* | high |
| *altopiano, altipiano* | high altitude plateau |
| *autostazione* | bus station |
| *balma* | primitive shepherds' dwellings with dry-stone walls |
| *becca, cima, punta, testa* | mountain peak, summit |
| *bivacco* | bivouac hut |
| *bocca, bocchetta, col, colle, finestra, fenêtre, passo* | mountain pass |
| *borgata, frazione, hameau* | hamlet |
| *cabinovia* | gondola lift |
| *caduta sassi* | falling rocks |
| *camere libere* | rooms available |
| *capanna, casotto* | hut |
| *capoluogo* | provincial or regional capital or town |
| *cascata* | waterfall |
| *casolare* | hut |
| *casotto PNGP* | park ranger's hut |
| *cengia* | ledge |
| *comba, combe* | long narrow valley |
| *costa* | flank, slope |
| *cresta* | crest, ridge |
| *dessot/dessus* | lower/upper |
| *diga* | dam |
| *est/orientale* | east/eastern |
| *facile* | easy |
| *finestra, fenêtre* | literally 'window', col, pass |
| *fiume* | river |
| *funivia* | cable-car |
| *ghiacciaio* | glacier |

## Gran Paradiso – Alta Via 2 Trek and Day Walks

| | |
|---|---|
| *grangia* | stone shepherd's hut, used seasonally |
| *lac (lacs), lago (laghi)* | lake (lakes) |
| *località* | place, locality |
| *mayen* | medium-altitude farm that can be utilised early (such as May, hence the name) to provide livestock with fresh grass |
| *montagna* | high altitude summer farm in Valle d'Aosta |
| *muanda* | high altitude summer farm in Piemonte |
| *nord/settentrionale* | north/northern |
| *ovest/occidentale* | west/western |
| *palestra di roccia* | rock-climbing area |
| *passeggiata* | promenade |
| *pedonale* | for pedestrians |
| *percorso* | route |
| *pericolo/pericoloso* | danger/dangerous |
| *piano* | plain, plateau when a noun (slowly or quietly, when an adverb) |
| *ponte* | bridge |
| *posto tappa* | hostel accommodation for walkers |
| *prato* | meadow |
| *Pro Loco* | local tourist office |
| *ricovero* | shelter |
| *ricovero invernale* | winter quarters adjoining a refuge |
| *rifugio* | mountain hut, usually manned |
| *rio, torrente* | mountain stream |
| *san, santo, santa* | saint |
| *seggiovia* | chair lift |
| *sentiero* | path |
| *soccorso alpino* | mountain rescue |
| *sorgente* | spring (water) |
| *stazione ferroviaria* | railway station |
| *sud/meridionale* | south/southern |
| *telecabina* | gondola car |
| *tornante* | hairpin bend |
| *torre* | tower |
| *torrente* | mountain stream |
| *traforo* | road tunnel |
| *val, valle, vallon, vallone* | valley |

# APPENDIX B
*Route Summary Table*

## Alta Via 2

| Stage | Time | Distance | Ascent/Descent | Grade |
|---|---|---|---|---|
| 1 | 2h45 | 5.8km | 738m/--------- | 1–2 |
| 2 | 3h | 7.8km | 636m/298m | 2 |
| 3 | 3h40 | 14.8km | ------/986m | 2 |
| 4 | 3h20 | 8.3km | 1050m/------ | 1–2 |
| 5 | 5h45 | 16.2km | 712m/1630m | 2–3 |
| 6 | 6h40 | 15.9km | 1341m/1284m | 2 |
| 7 | 3h30 | 7.4km | 1117m/470m | 2–3 |
| 8 | 3h30 | 13.4km | 148m/934m | 2 |
| 9 | 5h50 | 11km | 1284m/1189m | 2–3 |
| 10 | 7h15 | 16km | 1211m/1425m | 2 |
| 11 | 4h40 | 18.4km | 1156m/406m | 2 |
| 12 | 4h30 | 12.7km | 400m/1390m | 2 |
| **Totals** | **54h25** | **147.7km** | **9793m/10,012m** | |

## Walks

| Walk | Time | Distance | Ascent/Descent | Grade |
|---|---|---|---|---|
| 1 | 1h30 | 2.3km | 150m/150m | 1 |
| 2 | 4h45 | 10.1km | 760m/760m | 2 |
| 3 | 5h | 12km | 660m/660m | 2 |
| 4 | 7h20 | 19km | 1100m/1100m | 2–3 |
| 5 | 7h30 | 13km | 1600m/1600m | 3 |
| 6 | 5h10 | 11.4km | 1470m/1765m | 2–3 |
| 7 | 7h45 | 23.6km | 1230m/1480m | 2 |
| 8 | 6h20 | 19.8km | 1120m/1120m | 2 |
| 9 | 1h30 | 5.3km | --------/300m | 1 |
| 10 | 4h40 | 11km | 1050m/1050m | 1–2 |
| 11 | 6h | 16km | 1210m/1120m | 2 |
| 12 | 4h50 | 10.5km | 1090m/440m | 2 |
| 13 | 4h30 | 10.5km | 730m/730m | 2 |

## Walks continued

| Walk | Time | Distance | Ascent/Descent | Grade |
|------|------|----------|----------------|-------|
| 14 | 4h15 | 9km | 840m/840m | 2 |
| 15 | 6h | 17.5km | 570m/1450m | 2–3 |
| 16 | 7h | 18.7km | 1550m/660m | 3 |
| 17 | 11h15 | 33km | 1610m/1670m | 3 |
| 18 | 3h45 | 9.7km | 515m/515m | 2 |
| 19 | 5h30 | 14km | 1210m/1210m | 2–3 |
| 20 | 8h | 24km | 910m/1920m | 2–3 |
| 21 | 2h | 5.8km | 200m/200m | 1 |
| 22 | 6h30 | 14.7km | 1050m/1050m | 2 |
| 23 | 3h | 6.3km | 470m/470m | 1–2 |
| 24 | 2h15 | 5.3km | 410m/410m | 1–2 |
| 25 | 3h30 | 9.7km | 670m/670m | 2 |
| 26 | 6h | 12.4km | 1175m/1175m | 2 |
| 27 | 5h30 | 13.3km | 1050m/1050m | 2 |
| 28 | 5h | 10.8km | 1030m/1030m | 2 |

# LISTING OF CICERONE GUIDES

**SCOTLAND**

Backpacker's Britain:
    Northern Scotland
Ben Nevis and Glen Coe
Cycling in the Hebrides
Great Mountain Days in
    Scotland
Mountain Biking in Southern
    and Central Scotland
Mountain Biking in West and
    North West Scotland
Not the West Highland Way
    Scotland
Scotland's Best Small Mountains
Scotland's Far West
Scotland's Mountain Ridges
Scrambles in Lochaber
The Ayrshire and Arran
    Coastal Paths
The Border Country
The Cape Wrath Trail
The Great Glen Way
The Great Glen Way Map
    Booklet
The Hebridean Way
The Hebrides
The Isle of Mull
The Isle of Skye
The Skye Trail
The Southern Upland Way
The Speyside Way
The Speyside Way Map Booklet
The West Highland Way
Walking Highland Perthshire
Walking in Scotland's Far North
Walking in the Angus Glens
Walking in the Cairngorms
Walking in the Ochils, Campsie
    Fells and Lomond Hills
Walking in the Pentland Hills
Walking in the Southern
    Uplands
Walking in Torridon
Walking Loch Lomond and
    the Trossachs
Walking on Arran
Walking on Harris and Lewis
Walking on Jura, Islay
    and Colonsay
Walking on Rum and the
    Small Isles
Walking on the Orkney and
    Shetland Isles
Walking on Uist and Barra
Walking the Corbetts
    Vol 1 South of the Great Glen
Walking the Corbetts
    Vol 2 North of the Great Glen
Walking the Galloway Hills
Walking the Munros
    Vol 1 – Southern, Central and
    Western Highlands
Walking the Munros
    Vol 2 – Northern Highlands
    and the Cairngorms
West Highland Way Map
    Booklet
Winter Climbs Ben Nevis and
    Glen Coe
Winter Climbs in the Cairngorms

**NORTHERN ENGLAND TRAILS**

Hadrian's Wall Path
Hadrian's Wall Path Map
    Booklet
Pennine Way Map Booklet
The Coast to Coast Map Booklet
The Coast to Coast Walk
The Dales Way
The Pennine Way

**LAKE DISTRICT**

Cycling in the Lake District
Great Mountain Days in the
    Lake District
Lake District Winter Climbs
Lake District: High Level and
    Fell Walks
Lake District: Low Level and
    Lake Walks
Lakeland Fellranger series
Mountain Biking in the
    Lake District
Scrambles in the
    Lake District – North
Scrambles in the
    Lake District – South
Short Walks in Lakeland
    Books 1, 2 and 3
The Cumbria Coastal Way
The Cumbria Way
Tour of the Lake District
Trail and Fell Running in the
    Lake District

**NORTH WEST ENGLAND
AND THE ISLE OF MAN**

Cycling the Pennine Bridleway
Isle of Man Coastal Path
The Lancashire Cycleway
The Lune Valley and Howgills –
    A Walking Guide
The Ribble Way
Walking in Cumbria's Eden
    Valley
Walking in Lancashire
Walking in the Forest of
    Bowland and Pendle
Walking on the Isle of Man
Walking on the West
    Pennine Moors
Walks in Lancashire
    Witch Country
Walks in Ribble Country
Walks in Silverdale and Arnside
Walks in the Forest of Bowland

**NORTH EAST ENGLAND,
YORKSHIRE DALES
AND PENNINES**

Cycling in the Yorkshire Dales
Great Mountain Days in
    the Pennines
Historic Walks in North
    Yorkshire
Mountain Biking in the
    Yorkshire Dales
South Pennine Walks
St Oswald's Way and
    St Cuthbert's Way
The Cleveland Way and the
    Yorkshire Wolds Way
The Cleveland Way Map Booklet
The North York Moors
The Reivers Way
The Teesdale Way
Walking in County Durham
Walking in Northumberland
Walking in the North Pennines
Walking in the Yorkshire Dales:
    North and East
Walking in the Yorkshire Dales:
    South and West
Walks in Dales Country
Walks in the Yorkshire Dales

**WALES AND WELSH BORDERS**

Glyndwr's Way
Great Mountain Days
    in Snowdonia
Hillwalking in Shropshire
Hillwalking in Wales – Vol 1
Hillwalking in Wales – Vol 2
Mountain Walking in Snowdonia
Offa's Dyke Path
Offa's Dyke Map Booklet
Pembrokeshire Coast Path
    Map Booklet
Ridges of Snowdonia
Scrambles in Snowdonia
The Ascent of Snowdon
The Ceredigion and Snowdonia
    Coast Paths

The Pembrokeshire Coast Path
The Severn Way
The Snowdonia Way
The Wales Coast Path
The Wye Valley Walk
Walking in Carmarthenshire
Walking in Pembrokeshire
Walking in the Forest of Dean
Walking in the South
  Wales Valleys
Walking in the Wye Valley
Walking on the Brecon Beacons
Walking on the Gower
Welsh Winter Climbs

### DERBYSHIRE, PEAK DISTRICT AND MIDLANDS

Cycling in the Peak District
Dark Peak Walks
Scrambles in the Dark Peak
Walking in Derbyshire
White Peak Walks:
  The Northern Dales

### SOUTHERN ENGLAND

20 Classic Sportive Rides in South East England
20 Classic Sportive Rides in South West England
Cycling in the Cotswolds
Mountain Biking on the North Downs
Mountain Biking on the South Downs
North Downs Way Map Booklet
South West Coast Path Map Booklet – Minehead to St Ives
South West Coast Path Map Booklet – Plymouth to Poole
South West Coast Path Map Booklet – St Ives to Plymouth
Suffolk Coast and Heath Walks
The Cotswold Way
The Cotswold Way Map Booklet
The Great Stones Way
The Kennet and Avon Canal
The Lea Valley Walk
The North Downs Way
The Peddars Way and Norfolk Coast Path
The Pilgrims' Way
The Ridgeway Map Booklet
The Ridgeway National Trail
The South Downs Way
The South Downs Way Map Booklet
The South West Coast Path
The Thames Path
The Thames Path Map Booklet
The Two Moors Way
Walking in Cornwall
Walking in Essex
Walking in Kent
Walking in London
Walking in Norfolk
Walking in Sussex
Walking in the Chilterns
Walking in the Cotswolds
Walking in the Isles of Scilly
Walking in the New Forest
Walking in the North Wessex Downs
Walking in the Thames Valley
Walking on Dartmoor
Walking on Guernsey
Walking on Jersey
Walking on the Isle of Wight
Walking the Jurassic Coast
Walks in the South Downs National Park

### BRITISH ISLES CHALLENGES, COLLECTIONS AND ACTIVITIES

The Book of the Bivvy
The Book of the Bothy
The C2C Cycle Route
The End to End Cycle Route
The End to End Trail
The Mountains of England and Wales: Vol 1 Wales
The Mountains of England and Wales: Vol 2 England
The National Trails
The UK's County Tops
Three Peaks, Ten Tors

### ALPS CROSS-BORDER ROUTES

100 Hut Walks in the Alps
Across the Eastern Alps: E5
Alpine Ski Mountaineering Vol 1 – Western Alps
Alpine Ski Mountaineering Vol 2 – Central and Eastern Alps
Chamonix to Zermatt
The Tour of the Bernina
Tour of Mont Blanc
Tour of Monte Rosa
Tour of the Matterhorn
Trail Running – Chamonix and the Mont Blanc region
Trekking in the Alps
Trekking in the Silvretta and Rätikon Alps
Trekking Munich to Venice
Walking in the Alps

### PYRENEES AND FRANCE/SPAIN CROSS-BORDER ROUTES

The GR10 Trail
The GR11 Trail – La Senda
The Mountains of Andorra
The Pyrenean Haute Route
The Pyrenees
The Way of St James – France
The Way of St James – Spain
Walks and Climbs in the Pyrenees

### AUSTRIA

The Adlerweg
Trekking in Austria's Hohe Tauern
Trekking in the Stubai Alps
Trekking in the Zillertal Alps
Walking in Austria

### SWITZERLAND

Cycle Touring in Switzerland
The Swiss Alpine Pass Route – Via Alpina Route 1
The Swiss Alps
Tour of the Jungfrau Region
Walking in the Bernese Oberland
Walking in the Valais
Walks in the Engadine – Switzerland

### FRANCE

Chamonix Mountain Adventures
Cycle Touring in France
Cycling the Canal du Midi
Écrins National Park
Mont Blanc Walks
Mountain Adventures in the Maurienne
The Cathar Way
The GR20 Corsica
The GR5 Trail
The GR5 Trail – Vosges and Jura
The Grand Traverse of the Massif Central
The Loire Cycle Route
The Moselle Cycle Route
The River Rhone Cycle Route
The Robert Louis Stevenson Trail
Tour of the Oisans: The GR54
Tour of the Queyras
Tour of the Vanoise
Vanoise Ski Touring
Via Ferratas of the French Alps
Walking in Corsica
Walking in Provence – East
Walking in Provence – West
Walking in the Auvergne
Walking in the Cevennes
Walking in the Dordogne
Walking in the Haute Savoie: South
Walks in the Cathar Region
Walking in the Ardennes

### GERMANY
Hiking and Biking in the Black Forest
The Danube Cycleway Volume 1
The Rhine Cycle Route
The Westweg
Walking in the Bavarian Alps

### ICELAND AND GREENLAND
Trekking in Greenland
Walking and Trekking in Iceland

### IRELAND
The Irish Coast to Coast Walk
The Mountains of Ireland

### ITALY
Italy's Sibillini National Park
Shorter Walks in the Dolomites
Ski Touring and Snowshoeing in the Dolomites
The Way of St Francis
Through the Italian Alps
Trekking in the Apennines
Trekking in the Dolomites
Via Ferratas of the Italian Dolomites: Vol 1
Via Ferratas of the Italian Dolomites: Vol 2
Walking in Abruzzo
Walking in Italy's Stelvio National Park
Walking in Sardinia
Walking in Sicily
Walking in the Dolomites
Walking in Umbria
Walking on the Amalfi Coast
Walking the Italian Lakes
Walks and Treks in the Maritime Alps

### SCANDINAVIA
Walking in Norway

### EASTERN EUROPE AND THE BALKANS
The Danube Cycleway Volume 2
The High Tatras
The Mountains of Romania
Walking in Bulgaria's National Parks
Walking in Hungary
Mountain Biking in Slovenia
The Islands of Croatia
The Julian Alps of Slovenia
The Mountains of Montenegro
Trekking in Slovenia
Walking in Croatia
Walking in Slovenia: The Karavanke

### SPAIN
Coastal Walks in Andalucia
Cycle Touring in Spain
Mountain Walking in Southern Catalunya
Spain's Sendero Histórico: The GR1
The Mountains of Nerja
The Northern Caminos
The Sierras of Extremadura
The Way of St James Cyclist Guide
Trekking in Mallorca
Walking in Andalucia
Walking in Mallorca
Walking in Menorca
Walking in the Cordillera Cantabrica
Walking in the Sierra Nevada
Walking on Gran Canaria
Walking on La Gomera and El Hierro
Walking on La Palma
Walking on Lanzarote and Fuerteventura
Walking on Tenerife
Walking on the Costa Blanca
Walking the GR7 in Andalucia
Walks and Climbs in the Picos de Europa

### PORTUGAL
Walking in Madeira
Walking in the Algarve

### GREECE
The High Mountains of Crete
Walking and Trekking on Corfu

### CYPRUS
Walking in Cyprus

### MALTA
Walking on Malta

### INTERNATIONAL CHALLENGES, COLLECTIONS AND ACTIVITIES
Canyoning in the Alps
The Via Francigena Canterbury to Rome – Part 2

### AFRICA
Climbing in the Moroccan Anti-Atlas
Kilimanjaro: A Complete Trekker's Guide
Mountaineering in the Moroccan High Atlas
The High Atlas
Trekking in the Atlas Mountains
Walking in the Drakensberg

### ASIA
Jordan – Walks, Treks, Caves, Climbs and Canyons
Treks and Climbs in Wadi Rum, Jordan
Annapurna
Everest: A Trekker's Guide
Trekking in the Himalaya
Bhutan
Trekking in Ladakh
The Mount Kailash Trek

### NORTH AMERICA
British Columbia
The Grand Canyon
The John Muir Trail
The Pacific Crest Trail

### SOUTH AMERICA
Aconcagua and the Southern Andes
Hiking and Biking Peru's Inca Trails
Torres del Paine

### TECHNIQUES
Geocaching in the UK
Indoor Climbing
Lightweight Camping
Map and Compass
Outdoor Photography
Polar Exploration
Rock Climbing
Sport Climbing
The Hillwalker's Manual

### MINI GUIDES
Alpine Flowers
Avalanche!
Navigation
Pocket First Aid and Wilderness Medicine
Snow

### MOUNTAIN LITERATURE
8000 metres
A Walk in the Clouds
Abode of the Gods
The Pennine Way – the Path, the People, the Journey
Unjustifiable Risk?

For full information on all our guides, books and eBooks, visit our website:
**www.cicerone.co.uk**

**Walking – Trekking – Mountaineering – Climbing – Cycling**

**Over 40 years, Cicerone have built up an outstanding collection of over 300 guides, inspiring all sorts of amazing adventures.**

Every guide comes from extensive exploration and research by our expert authors, all with a passion for their subjects. They are frequently praised, endorsed and used by clubs, instructors and outdoor organisations.

All our titles can now be bought as **e-books**, **ePubs** and **Kindle** files and we also have an online magazine – **Cicerone Extra** – with features to help cyclists, climbers, walkers and trekkers choose their next adventure, at home or abroad.

Our website shows any **new information** we've had in since a book was published. Please do let us know if you find anything has changed, so that we can publish the latest details. On our **website** you'll also find great ideas and lots of detailed information about what's inside every guide and you can buy **individual routes** from many of them online.

It's easy to keep in touch with what's going on at Cicerone by getting our monthly **free e-newsletter**, which is full of offers, competitions, up-to-date information and topical articles. You can subscribe on our home page and also follow us on **Facebook** and **Twitter** or dip into our **blog**.

**Cicerone – the very best guides for exploring the world.**

## CICERONE

Juniper House, Murley Moss, Oxenholme Road, Kendal, Cumbria LA9 7RL
Tel: 015395 62069  info@cicerone.co.uk
**www.cicerone.co.uk** and **www.cicerone-extra.com**